# DIAMOND DAYS

## A HISTORY OF
## THE KING GEORGE VI
## AND QUEEN ELIZABETH
## DIAMOND STAKES

# DIAMOND DAYS

—— A HISTORY OF ——
## THE KING GEORGE VI AND QUEEN ELIZABETH DIAMOND STAKES

## Stephen Michael Brie

Hodder & Stoughton
LONDON SYDNEY AUCKLAND TORONTO

# For Paula

The author is grateful to the proprietors of Timeform for allowing the use of their ratings.

British Library Cataloguing in Publication Data

Brie, Stephen Michael
  Diamond days: a history of the King George VI and
  Queen Elizabeth Diamond Stakes
  1. Racehorses. Racing. Races, story
  I. Title
  798.4009

  ISBN 0-340-52525-8

First published in Great Britain 1990

Published by Hodder and Stoughton,
a division of Hodder and Stoughton Ltd,
Mill Road, Dunton Green, Sevenoaks, Kent TN13 2YA.
Editorial Office: 47 Bedford Square, London WC1B 3DP.

Photoset by Rowland Phototypesetting Ltd,
Bury St Edmunds, Suffolk

Printed in Great Britain by Butler and Tanner Ltd,
Frome and London

# Contents

# Illustrations

[1] Hulton-Deutsch Collection
[2] Sporting Pictures UK Ltd
[3] Bernard Parkin
[4] Paddock Studios
[5] W. Baybutt

# INTRODUCTION

It is a Saturday afternoon in late July and ideally the sun is beating down upon the green expanse of Ascot racecourse. The faithful have gathered from near and far to worship the majesty of the thorough-bred and the high summer air is heavy with anticipation.

The field of equine aristocrats powers its way down to the twelve-furlong start – a rainbow of silk stretching across the track atop gleaming, muscular flanks. The time is twenty past three – the last horse is installed – the starter raises his flag and the stalls crash open. At once there is a release of awe-inspiring power – an explosion of speed which sends the dash for the Diamonds on its way.

Now firmly established as Britain's most important middle-distance weight-for-age contest, the King George VI and Queen Elizabeth Diamond Stakes was the brainchild of Ascot Clerk of the Course Sir John Crocker Bulteel. With assistance from His Majesty's Ascot Representative, the 16th Duke of Norfolk, Sir John formulated the new race as racing's contribution to the 1951 Festival of Britain. The King George VI and Queen Elizabeth Festival of Britain Stakes, as it was originally titled, incorporated the King George Stakes and the Queen Elizabeth Stakes, both former features of the Ascot programme. "Festival of Britain" was dropped from the race title in 1952, and the word "Diamond" added in 1975, in recognition of De Beers Consolidated Mines Limited, race sponsors since 1972.

The new race, for three-year-olds and upwards, over the Derby and Oaks distance of twelve furlongs, was an instant success and soon rivalled the Prix de l'Arc de Triomphe as Europe's middle-distance championship.

Over the past four decades the King George has been won in spectacular fashion by such legendary names as PINZA, RIBOT, NIJINSKY, MILL REEF and BRIGADIER GERARD. We have witnessed titanic, blood-stirring, head to head finishes such as those between GRUNDY and Bustino and NASHWAN and Cacoethes, and we have watched in astonishment as the supposed "certainties", Petite Etoile and Santa Claus were well and truly turned over.

At the time of writing, thirty-eight horses have earned immortality by landing the King George, DAHLIA being the only dual winner. This book is a tribute to those who fought and won on those historic "Diamond Days".

# 1951

From an original entry of ninety-six, the King George VI and Queen Elizabeth Festival of Britain Stakes attracted a large field of nineteen, a figure which has, to date, never been surpassed. The field was rich in quality as well as quantity, with five Classic winners and an Arc winner coming under starter's orders.

On a gloriously sunny July day, the Queen and Princess Elizabeth saw the three-year-old SUPREME COURT land the richest prize ever contested on any racecourse in this country.

Amazingly SUPREME COURT had been rejected as a yearling by two of the most distinguished trainers in the land, Noel Murless and Marcus Marsh. Although he is officially listed as being by either Persian Gulf or Precipitation, he was almost certainly the product of the union between the latter stallion and the mare Forecourt. A rather leggy yearling, he was offered to both Murless and Marsh, but neither trainer was able to find room for the colt. His owner, Mrs Vera Lilley, eventually placed SUPREME COURT with Evan Williams at Kingsclere. Williams, who had ridden Royal Mail to victory in the 1937 Grand National, immediately struck up an understanding with the big brown colt.

Williams brought the gangly SUPREME COURT along slowly, giving him just three outings as a juvenile. After showing promise in his first two races, both at Ascot, SUPREME COURT lost his maiden tag with a convincing three-length success in the valuable Horris Hill Stakes at Newbury. His connections were confident that the colt would develop into an even better three-year-old.

SUPREME COURT reappeared in the White Lodge Stakes over a mile at Hurst Park, where he had little more than an exercise canter to dispose of his twelve rivals and just over two weeks later, he put up a brilliant performance in the Chester Vase. Under an inspired ride from Australian Rae Johnstone, the colt produced an electrifying burst of acceleration which took him from last to first in a matter of strides. Williams was now certain that he had a real racehorse on his hands.

The winning sequence was maintained in the King Edward VII Stakes at Royal Ascot, where Williams's charge gave four pounds and a length beating to the useful Sybil's Nephew.

The canny Kingsclere trainer now turned his attention to the vast purse up for grabs in the newly framed King George. Could Mrs Lilley's "reject" beat the best horses in Europe at Ascot? Despite his impressive string of victories, SUPREME COURT was only fourth favourite to land the new race.

The 1951 Derby winner Arctic Prince headed the market. The Prince Chevalier colt had looked top-class when coasting home by six lengths at Epsom. The Ascot race would provide Willie Stephenson's horse with the chance to take on his elders for the first time.

Leading the four-year-old challenge was the French-bred Tantième. Winner of both the Poule d'Essai des Poulains and the Prix de l'Arc de Triomphe in 1950, Tantième had already captured a major English prize in the shape of the 1951 Coronation Cup. François Mathet's charge was sent off the 7–2 second favourite at Ascot. Of the other five French challengers, only the 1950 St Leger winner Scratch II appeared good enough to trouble the home contingent.

Apart from Arctic Prince and SUPREME COURT, three other English-trained candidates held strong claims.

Winston Churchill's grey, Colonist II, had made all the running to land both the Winston Churchill Stakes and the White Rose Stakes. It seemed likely, however, that the colt needed further than twelve furlongs to show his best form, and many observers believed he would struggle to keep pace with some of his more speedy rivals at Ascot. Nevertheless, he was not without support at 100–7.

Zucchero, the mount of fifteen-year-old Lester Piggott, had chalked up four victories in the first half of the season. The Nasrullah colt was, however, a rather temperamental individual, and not the type to trust with the family savings.

The other serious contender was the filly Belle Of All, on whom Gordon Richards put up one pound overweight. Winner of the One Thousand Guineas, Belle Of All was expected to run with distinction, and attracted a fair amount of support in the ring. The other

Classic winner in the field, the Two Thousand Guineas winner Ki Ming, was not thought to have the necessary stamina to cope with the stiff Ascot mile and a half.

Under a cloudless sky, the nineteen runners set off at a furious pace, with Mossborough, Belle Of All and Tantième disputing the early lead. After three furlongs, Manny Mercer pushed Wilwyn up to join the leaders. In behind, Elliott and Piggott settled their mounts just off the pace. As the field turned into the home straight, the punishing pace had taken its toll on Mossborough and Belle Of All, leaving Tantième at the head of affairs. With two furlongs to run, the French colt started to hang left towards the stand side, leaving a gap through which Arctic Prince, SUPREME COURT and Zucchero all passed.

Suddenly Arctic Prince began to falter, leaving Elliott and Piggott to fight out the finish and at the furlong pole SUPREME COURT hit the front. Under strong driving from his young pilot, Zucchero desperately struggled to peg back his rival. With whips flying, SUPREME COURT passed the post three-quarters of a length ahead of Zucchero, with Tantième a further six lengths back in third. Colonist II, who ran on well in the closing stages, finished a gallant fourth. The favourite, Arctic Prince, was found to have broken down over a furlong out. As expected, the time was extremely fast, beating the previous course record by 0.2 seconds. With huge crowds, royal patronage, and a terrific finish, the new race was deemed an outstanding success.

SUPREME COURT did not race again after Ascot. He retired to the Banstead Manor Stud near Newmarket, the winner of five of his eight races. He died in 1962. The pick of his offspring was probably Middle Park Stakes winner Pipe of Peace. SUPREME COURT's daughters have made excellent brood mares, and include the dams of Hopeful Venture and of Rheingold.

## 1951

### KING GEORGE VI AND QUEEN ELIZABETH FESTIVAL OF BRITAIN STAKES

£25,322 10s     1m 4f

July 21, 1951

| | | | |
|---|---|---|---|
| 1 | SUPREME COURT | 3 8–4 | E. C. Elliott. br.c. by Persian Gulf or Precipitation–Forecourt |
| 2 | ZUCCHERO | 3 8–4 | L. Piggott. br.c. by Nasrullah–Castagnola |
| 3 | TANTIÈME (FR) | 4 9–4 | J. Doyasbere. b.c. by Deux Pour Cent–Terka |
| 4 | COLONIST II | 5 9–4 | T. Gosling. gr.h. by Rienzo–Cybele |
| 5 | MOSSBOROUGH | 4 9–4 | D. Smith. ch.c. by Nearco–All Moonshine |
| 6 | OLEIN'S GRACE | 5 9–4 | M. Molony. br.h. by His Grace–Sweet and Rough |
| 7 | KELLING | 4 9–4 | E. Smith. ch.c. by Orestes–Monk's Fancy |
| 8 | ARCTIC PRINCE | 3 8–4 | C. Spares. br.c. by Prince Chevalier–Arctic Sun |
| 9 | STENIGOT | 4 9–4 | A. Breasley. b.c. by Bois Roussel–Par Excellence |
| 10 | BURNT BROWN | 5 9–4 | W. Evans. b.h. by the Phoenix–Suntop |
| 11 | SCRATCH II (FR) | 4 9–4 | W. Johnstone. ch.c. by Pharis–Orlamonde |
| 12 | LE TYROL (FR) | 3 8–4 | M. Lollierou. b.c. by Verso II–Princess Lointaine II |
| 13 | AQUINO II (FR) | 3 8–4 | C. Bouillon. b.c. by Tornado–Apulia |
| 14 | BELLE OF ALL | 3 8–2 | G. Richards. b.f. by Nasrullah–Village Beauty |
| 15 | DYNAMITER (FR) | 3 8–5 | C. Poincelet. br.c. by Pharis II–Pretty Lady |
| 16 | CORSAIR IV (FR) | 3 8–4 | M. Quemet. b.c. by Caracalla II–Fama |
| 17 | WILWYN | 3 8–4 | E. Mercer. b.c. by Pink Flower–Saracen |
| 18 | KI MING | 3 8–4 | K. Gethin. br.c. by Ballyogan–Ulster Lily |
| 19 | HIGHCREST | 3 8–4 | G. Littlewood, ch.c. by River Prince–Lady Turk |

19 Ran

Going – Good

Distances: ¾,6,1½,2,hd

Time: 2:29.4

S.P. 100–30 ARCTIC PRINCE, 7–2 TANTIÈME, 10–1 SCRATCH II, 100–9 SUPREME COURT, 12–1 ZUCCHERO, BELLE OF ALL, 100–7 COLONIST II, 20–1 DYNAMITER, WILWYN, AQUINO II, 33–1 OLEIN'S GRACE, MOSSBOROUGH, 50–1 KELLING, KI MING, 66–1 LE TYROL, 100–1 OTHERS

Winner trained by E. Williams at Kingsclere: owned by Mrs T. Lilley: bred by Mr T. Lilley

Timeform rating of winner 135

# 1952

I n 1952 the French sent a seven-strong raiding party to Ascot in an attempt to take the £23,302 10s first prize across the English Channel. In the event, the Gallic challengers were hopelessly outclassed by the three-year-old champion of England, TULYAR.

Owned and bred by the Aga Khan, TULYAR completed his juvenile season without attracting too much attention. The winner of two ordinary mile races from his six outings, TULYAR was considered by trainer Marcus Marsh to be a potentially useful long-distance handicapper. Stable jockey Charlie Smirke also rated the son of Tehran below Classic standard. In his autobiography, *Finishing Post*, Smirke wrote of his hopes of one day winning the Cesarewitch with the colt. Indeed, so lazy was TULYAR at home, that even the stable's lesser lights were able to beat him on the Newmarket gallops.

It was not until the colt had won the Ormonde Stakes at Chester that connections began to see him as a potential Classic winner. TULYAR arrived at Chester having won his first outing as a three-year-old, the Henry VIII Stakes at Hurst Park. Smirke, who fought a running battle with the scales throughout his career, was unable to make the weight of seven stone, nine pounds at Chester, and so Doug Smith was given the mount. After hitting the front at the distance, the combination had little difficulty in beating the useful Nikiforos by half a length.

After coasting home in the Lingfield Derby Trial, Marsh decided to let TULYAR take his chance at Epsom. Sent off the 11–2 favourite, TULYAR took the lead two furlongs out, and comfortably held the challenge of Gay Time by three-quarters of a length. After the race an ebullient Smirke greeted the assembled ranks of the press with the now famous quip, "What did I Tulyar?" The one-time Cesarewitch hope had landed the Blue Riband of the English Turf.

TULYAR's last race prior to the King George was in the Eclipse Stakes at Sandown, where the colt accounted for stable companion Mehmandar in a hack canter. Seven days later TULYAR faced the starter at Ascot, a well supported favourite at 3–1. As usual Smirke had to struggle to make the weight. Despite spending every available moment in the Turkish baths, he was forced to put up two pounds overweight at eight stone, six pounds.

TULYAR's closest market rival was the four-year-old Zucchero. Doug Smith's mount was attempting to improve on his second place in the 1951 King George. Often a temperamental individual, Zucchero had been on his best behaviour when recording his first victory of 1952 in the Princess of Wales's Stakes at Newmarket, two weeks prior to the King George. Lester Piggott, who had partnered Zucchero in 1951, opted to ride Noel Murless's Gay Time. Strictly on form, the Warren Place colt had a chance to gain revenge on TULYAR for a three-quarter length beating in the Derby. With Smirke putting up two pounds overweight at Ascot, Murless was confident of a bold show from his charge.

Of the seven French raiders, only Nuccio had a realistic chance of landing the spoils. The four-year-old had already proved his ability to adapt to English conditions with a comfortable victory over Sybil's Nephew in the Coronation Cup at Epsom. Harry Wragg's four-year-old Fraise Du Bois was an interesting runner. Winner of the Irish Derby in 1951, he was well fancied by his connections, despite a poor showing behind TULYAR in the Eclipse Stakes. On Sandown form Fraise Du Bois had six and a half lengths to make up on the favourite.

As the large Ascot crowd basked in brilliant sunshine, a drama began to unfold down at the start. The French-trained Mat de Cocagne kicked out violently, catching Zucchero just above the knee. With Doug Smith's mount in need of attention, and Mat de Cocagne giving a passable impression of a mad bull elephant, the start was delayed for almost ten minutes. When the tapes eventually went up Mat de Cocagne continued his performance, virtually pulling himself up after half a furlong.

The first to show was Le Sage, the mount of Gordon Richards, closely followed by Gay Time, Sybil's Nephew and TULYAR. Turning into the straight, the order remained the same, although Worden II looked to be going ominously well in fifth place. Smirke was well aware of the danger posed by the Gallic raider looming up on TULYAR's inside. Quite deliberately, and quite legitimately, he eased his mount closer to the rails, thus closing the gap on Worden II. Bougoure was forced to check his mount and switch him to the outside to continue his challenge.

With two furlongs to run, Gay Time had the call, but both TULYAR and Worden II were poised to challenge. At the distance Smirke kicked TULYAR into the lead. In behind Worden II's effort proved short-lived, and it was left to Gay Time to chase home the favourite. Inside the last hundred yards, Piggott conjured a final spurt from Gay Time, but TULYAR always had the upper hand. At the line only a neck separated first and second, but TULYAR appeared to have won a shade cleverly. Worden II stayed on in his own time to take third place, just ahead of Le Sage. Zucchero, who was probably feeling the effects of his pre-race confrontation, ran a lifeless race and beat only two of his rivals.

TULYAR raced on one further occasion after Ascot, easily landing his second Classic of the season with a three-length success over Kingsfold in the St Leger.

Trainer Marcus Marsh would look back on the 1952 season with mixed feelings. Although TULYAR helped the Aga Khan to his thirteenth owner's title, and contributed to Marsh's position as leading trainer, the master of Fitzroy House lost all the Aga's horses to French stables at the close of the season.

The Aga Khan initially stated that TULYAR would remain in training as a four-year-old, but later changed his mind, and sold the colt to the Irish National Stud for a record £250,000. In 1955 TULYAR was resold to an American syndicate to stand at Claiborne Stud Farm in Kentucky. Although he never achieved outstanding success as a stallion, TULYAR did sire the Poule d'Essai des Pouliches winner Ginetta, and the Irish One Thousand Guineas winner Fiorentina.

# 1952

## KING GEORGE VI AND QUEEN ELIZABETH STAKES

£23,302 10s    1m 4f

July 19, 1952

| | | | |
|---|---|---|---|
| 1 | TULYAR | 3 8–6 | C. Smirke. br.c. by Tehran–Neocracy |
| 2 | GAY TIME | 3 8–4 | L. Piggott. ch.c. by Rockefella–Daring Miss |
| 3 | WORDEN II (FR) | 3 8–4 | G. Bougoure. ch.c. by Wild Risk–Sans Tares |
| 4 | LE SAGE | 4 9–4 | G. Richards. b.c. by Chamossaire–Miss Know All |
| 5 | H.V.C. | 3 8–7 | T. Gosling. ch.c. by Torbido–Shelton |
| 6 | ARBELE II (FR) | 3 8–1 | W. Johnstone, ch.f. by Djebel–Astronomie |
| 7 | EPICEA II (FR) | 3 8–4 | H. Signoret. b.c. by Eble–Platiname |
| 8 | SYBIL'S NEPHEW | 4 9–4 | W. Rickaby. b.c. by Honeyway or Midas–Sybil's Sister |
| 9 | NUCCIO (FR) | 4 9–4 | R. Poincelet. b.c. by Traghetto–Nuvoletta |
| 10 | NIEDERLANDER (GER) | 5 9–4 | O. Schmidt. br.h. by Ticino–Najade |
| 11 | L'AMIRAL (FR) | 5 9–4 | E. C. Elliott. br.h. by Admiral Drake–Hurrylor |
| 12 | FRAISE DU BOIS II | 4 9–4 | E. Mercer. b.c. by Bois Roussel–Sugar Hills |
| 13 | ZUCCHERO | 4 9–4 | D. Smith. br.c. by Nasrullah–Castagnola |
| 14 | MAT DE COCAGNE (FR) | 4 9–4 | C. Maire. b.c. by Birkil–Fascine II |
| 15 | LE BOURGEOIS (FR) | 3 8–4 | K. Gethin. b.c. by Vatelloe–Chatelaine |

15 Ran

Going – Good

Distances: nk,1½,1½,3,hd

Time: 2:33.2

[ 11 ]

S.P. 3–1 TULYAR, 7–1 ZUCCHERO, 15–2 GAY TIME, 8–1 LE SAGE, 100–9 NUCCIO, MAT DE COCAGNE, ARBELE II, 12–1 FRAISE DU BOIS II, 20–1 EPICEA II, 25–1 WORDEN II, L'AMIRAL, SYBIL'S NEPHEW, 33–1 H.V.C., 66–1 OTHERS

Winner trained by Marcus Marsh at Newmarket: owned by H. H. Aga Khan: bred by owner

Timeform rating of winner 134

# 1953

PINZA emerged from the 1953 season as both a hero and a villain. In Coronation Year, his victories in the Derby and the King George proved conclusively that he was the best horse in Europe, but both were gained at the expense of Her Majesty's Aureole.

Bred by Fred Darling, PINZA was purchased by Sir Victor Sassoon for 1,500 guineas at the Newmarket July Sales. By Chanteur II out of a Donatello II mare, he was a handsome heavy-topped individual with a distinctive broad white blaze.

Under the watchful eye of Newmarket trainer Norman Bertie, PINZA soon emerged as one of the top two-year-olds of 1952. After a quiet introduction at Hurst Park, PINZA scored his first victory in the Tattersalls Stakes at Doncaster, where, despite running green, he cruised home by six lengths. Bertie's colt was then surprisingly beaten in the Royal Lodge Stakes at Ascot. Sent off the 2–5 favourite, PINZA was under pressure fully two furlongs out, and had no answer to the challenge of the Charlie Smirke-ridden Neemah, who beat him by a length and a half. But in hammering Swashbuckler by five lengths in the Dewhurst Stakes on his final appearance as a two-year-old, PINZA more than made up for his disappointing Ascot display. At the close of the season he was allotted nine stone, two pounds in the Free Handicap, five pounds below the top-rated colt Nearula.

A powerful, masculine colt, PINZA was always something of a handful at home. During the winter he slipped on the road and damaged his shoulder, an injury which prevented his participation in the Two Thousand Guineas. With his usual partner Gordon Richards aboard, PINZA made a belated seasonal reappearance in the Newmarket Stakes in the middle of May. Looking none the worse for his enforced lay-off, the colt spreadeagled his field in breathtaking fashion, sauntering home four lengths clear of Polynesian. Prior to the race, PINZA had been quoted at 33–1 for the Derby, but unsurprisingly those odds soon disappeared.

The 1953 Epsom Derby was one of the most emotional events in Turf history. The race developed into a match between the newly crowned Queen's Aureole, and the newly knighted Sir Gordon Richards's mount PINZA. Richards had ridden in the Derby twenty-seven times without success. Could the big horse provide him with the one prize he so desperately coveted? Fate granted his wish. Taking the lead two furlongs out, the 5–1 joint favourite easily held Aureole's late challenge, coming home with four lengths to spare over the Queen's horse. The result was one of the most popular in the history of the Derby, and Sir Gordon and his gallant partner were given a deafening reception in the winner's circle. Sportingly, Her Majesty was one of the first to congratulate PINZA's connections.

And so to Ascot and the King George, where the Derby winner had to face twelve opponents.

Aureole, supported by the Queen, the Queen Mother and Princess Margaret, sought to reverse Epsom placings – a task which appeared to be beyond him without any weight concession from PINZA. The Two Thousand Guineas winner Nearula, the 5–1 second favourite at Ascot, had looked to be a non-stayer when trailing home in ninth place in the Derby. His victory over a mile in the St James's Palace Stakes, although impressive, had done little to prove his ability to handle twelve furlongs. The enigmatic Zucchero, now a five-year-old, was contesting the race for the third successive year. Second in 1951, and a remote thirteenth in 1952, he would need to be on his best behaviour if he were to trouble PINZA. The signs were not good however, as Piggott's mount had already refused to race at both Newmarket and Birmingham. When Zucchero was in the mood, as at Epsom where he won the Coronation Cup, he was a high-class performer. Those who took the 8–1 on offer at Ascot were either extremely brave or extremely foolish.

Best of the French challengers appeared to be Worden II, second in the race twelve months earlier, while the Italians sent two representatives, Alberigo, and his pacemaker Telemaco. Alberigo, a plain wiry type, had won the Italian Two Thousand Guineas, and been second in the Italian Derby. The Traghetto colt was something of an unknown quantity to English racegoers, and found little support at 20–1.

For the second successive year there was drama before the race. As the horses were leaving the paddock, the French colt Pharel lashed out and caught Aureole in the ribs. The royal colt reared up and threw Harry Carr to the ground. Thankfully neither horse nor jockey were seriously hurt and they were able to join the other horses in the parade.

Due to his immense power and sometimes nervous disposition, PINZA had two lads to attend to him in the parade ring, one leading him up, and one in the saddle. Despite their care, the colt was heavily bathed in sweat as he paraded in front of the packed Ascot stands.

After a false start caused by Nuccio rushing the tapes, the race eventually got under way. Zucchero, in one of his darker moods, decided he had had enough exercise for the day, and refused to jump off. With both Piggott and his trainer Payne employing maximum persuasion, Zucchero finally sulked into the race, a full furlong behind the rest of the field where he remained throughout the race.

Up ahead the enthusiastic runners were getting on with the race. In the early stages, Nuccio dictated the pace, followed by PINZA, Telemaco and Alberigo. Rounding the home bend, Richards let out an inch of rein and PINZA drew alongside Nuccio. Behind the two leaders, both Aureole and Worden II were making significant progress. At the two furlong pole PINZA swept into the lead. As Richards made the best of his way home, only Aureole and Worden II were within striking distance. Yet no strike materialised. As Richards pushed his mount out with hands and heels, Worden II's stride began to shorten, leaving Aureole to chase home the favourite. At the line PINZA was three lengths clear, a distance which Richards could have extended had he so wished.

PINZA had proved himself the best colt in Europe, and seemed to have the St Leger at his mercy. Unfortunately the colt damaged a tendon during his preparation and was unable to run. The King George proved to be PINZA's last race.

As a sire PINZA was something of a disappointment. His best offspring was probably Pinturischio who was ante post favourite for the 1961 Derby before being "got at". PINZA died in 1977.

# 1953

## KING GEORGE VI AND QUEEN ELIZABETH STAKES

£23,175    1m 4f

July 18, 1953

| 1 PINZA | 3 8–4 | Sir G. Richards. b.c. by Chanteur II–Pasqua |
|---|---|---|
| 2 AUREOLE | 3 8–4 | W. Carr. ch.c. by Hyperion–Angelola |
| 3 WORDEN II (FR) | 4 9–4 | C. Smirke. ch.c. by Wild Risk–Sans Tares |
| 4 PHAREL (FR) | 3 8–4 | D. Smith. b.c. by Djebel–Pharelle |
| 5 NUCCIO (FR) (b) | 5 9–4 | R. Poincelet. b.h. by Traghetto–Nuvoletta |
| 6 VAMOS (FR) | 4 9–4 | W. Johnstone. b.c. by Vatellor–Start Point |
| 7 SILNET (FR) | 4 9–4 | M. Larraun. b.c. by Fastnet–Silver Jill |
| 8 ALBERIGO (ITY) | 3 8–4 | S. Parravani. b.c. by Traghetto–Allerta |
| 9 KING OF THE TUDORS | 3 8–4 | C. Spares. ch.c. by Tudor Minstrel–Glen Line |
| 10 WILWYN | 5 9–4 | E. Mercer. b.h. by Pink Flower–Saracen |
| 11 NEARULA | 3 8–4 | E. Britt. b.c. by Nasrullah–Respite |
| 12 TELEMACO (ITY) | 3 8–4 | P. Caprioli. ch.c. by Traghetto–Teresa Muratori |
| 13 ZUCCHERO | 5 9–4 | L. Piggott. br.h. by Nasrullah–Castagnola |

13 Ran

Going – Good

Distances: 3,3,hd,½,3

Time: 2:33.6

S.P. 2–1 PINZA, 5–1 NEARULA, 15–2 NUCCIO, 18–1 ZUCCHERO, 100–9 WORDEN II, 100–7 WILWYN, 20–1 AUREOLE, VAMOS, ALBERIGO, 25–1 PHAREL, 33–1 SILNET, 50–1 others

Winner trained by Norman Bertie at Newmarket: owned by Sir Victor Sassoon: bred by Mr F. Darling

Timeform rating of winner 137

# 1954

With Pinza enjoying the stallion's life in 1954, his old rival AUREOLE was able to harvest the rich pickings on offer in the top middle-distance races.

Bred by the late King George VI, AUREOLE raced in the colours of Her Majesty Queen Elizabeth II. By the great Hyperion out of the Yorkshire Cup winner Angelola, he was a lovely bright chestnut with three white socks and a slashing white blaze.

In common with most Hyperions, AUREOLE was a highly strung individual. His trainer, Cecil Boyd-Rochfort, handled this bundle of dynamite with extreme skill and patience. Although the master of Freemason Lodge managed to rid the colt of his dislike of the starting gate, he was never able to find an answer to AUREOLE's aversion to the Limekilns, one of Newmarket's most popular gallops.

AUREOLE ran twice as a two-year-old. Having landed the Acomb Stakes at York on his debut, he finished sixth of nine in the Middle Park Stakes, after missing the break.

In his second season, the royal colt turned in a series of top-class performances. Although he won both the Lingfield Derby Trial and the Cumberland Lodge Stakes, his best efforts came in defeat. After finishing a close fifth in the Two Thousand Guineas, AUREOLE beat all but Pinza in a memorable finish to the Epsom Derby. The chestnut then took third place in the Eclipse Stakes, before again chasing home Pinza in the King George. He ended his three-year-old season in the St Leger, where he finished third behind his stable companion Premonition. During the winter, Boyd-Rochfort engaged the help of top London neurologist Charles Brook, who, using massage treatment, was able to calm considerably AUREOLE's nervous disposition.

The colt reappeared in the Coronation Stakes at Sandown, where he ran on to finish second behind Chamier, having suffered severe interference in the early stages of the race. Stable jockey Harry Carr, who did not get on with AUREOLE, was replaced at Sandown by Eph Smith. Smith, who had ridden the colt to win the Cumberland Lodge Stakes on his final outing of 1953, retained the ride for the remainder of the season.

AUREOLE's next racecourse test came in the Victor Wild Stakes at Kempton, where he had little difficulty in accounting for Westinform by four lengths, and the colt was even more impressive in landing the Coronation Cup at Epsom. Taking command three out, AUREOLE soon had his rivals toiling in his wake, running out a five-length winner from Chatsworth, with Nearula a further five lengths back in third.

The winning run continued in the Hardwicke Stakes at Royal Ascot. In a desperately close finish, Her Majesty's chestnut, conceding seven pounds, just held the late challenge of the French raider Janitor by the shortest of short heads. The pair were due to renew rivalry in the King George, where they would meet at level weights.

The 1954 King George was run on ground officially described as "dead". Most observers believed that AUREOLE would not be inconvenienced by the conditions, and he was sent off the 9–2 favourite. AUREOLE's main market rival was the Italian challenger Botticelli. A rather leggy Blue Peter colt, Botticelli had virtually swept the board in his home country, with victories in the Italian Two Thousand Guineas, the Italian Derby, the Gran Premio d'Italia, and the Gran Premio di Milano. He was well supported at Ascot, shortening from 8–1 to 5–1 prior to the off. As AUREOLE had already beaten Janitor, the best of the four French challengers, the chances of the prize ending up in France looked remote.

Ironically, one of the main dangers to AUREOLE appeared to be stable companion Premonition: Harry Carr's mount had beaten the royal colt in the 1953 St Leger. Successful in both the Yorkshire Cup and the Winston Churchill Stakes, Premonition would not be found lacking in stamina on the testing Ascot going. The Noel Murless-trained pair, Elopement and Rashleigh, and Harry Wragg's Two Thousand Guineas winner Darius were also expected to figure in the shake-up.

As the runners made their way down to the start, AUREOLE took offence to a rather gaudy umbrella, shied, and deposited Smith on the soggy Ascot turf. Thankfully neither horse nor jockey was injured, and they arrived down at the start without further incident.

As usual, AUREOLE was slowly away. After a furlong only the 33–1 chance Golden God was behind the favourite. Smith gave his mount plenty of time to recover the lost ground, and by the halfway stage he had joined the leading group, made up of Chatsworth, Savoyard II, and Darius.

Turning into the straight, AUREOLE was lying second, having overhauled the weakening Chatsworth. Smith kicked AUREOLE into the lead at the two furlong marker as Savoyard II dropped out of contention, leaving Darius and the fast finishing Vamos the only dangers. Vamos, who had finished sixth twelve months earlier, looked a big threat at the furlong pole. But, with Smith administering several sharp reminders inside the last hundred yards, the chestnut fought bravely to maintain his advantage. As the patriotic Ascot crowd spontaneously filled the sky with a multitude of flying hats, AUREOLE crossed the line three-quarters of a length ahead of Vamos, with the Guineas winner Darius a further two lengths back in third. The Italian hope, Botticelli, ran on well in the closing stages to finish sixth.

At the close of the season, AUREOLE's exploits allowed Her Majesty to top the owners list and contributed to Boyd-Rochfort's third trainer's title.

Certainly the best horse to carry the royal colours since the great Sun Chariot, AUREOLE took up stallion duties at Sandringham after the King George. An extremely successful sire, he was responsible for the 1960 Derby winner St Paddy; the 1961 St Leger winner Aurelius; and the 1965 St Leger winner Provoke. He died in 1975 at the grand old age of twenty-five.

## 1954

### KING GEORGE VI AND QUEEN ELIZABETH STAKES

£23,302     1m 4f

July 17, 1954

| 1 | AUREOLE | 4 9–4 | E. Smith. ch.c. by Hyperion–Angelola |
|---|---|---|---|
| 2 | VAMOS (FR) | 5 9–4 | R. Poincelet. b.h. by Vatellor–Start Point |
| 3 | DARIUS | 3 8–4 | F. Durr. b.c. by Dante–Yasna |
| 4 | SOUPEI | 6 9–4 | W. Johnstone. br.h. by Epigram–Sousse |
| 5 | ELOPEMENT | 3 8–4 | K. Gethin. ch.c. by Rockefella–Daring Miss |
| 6 | BOTTICELLI (ITY) | 3 8–4 | E. Camici. b.c. by Blue Peter–Buonamica |
| 7 | SAVOYARD (FR) | 4 9–4 | M. Quemet. b.c. by Un Gaillard–Sofia |
| 8 | CHAMIER | 4 9–4 | J. Mercer. ch.c. by Chamossaire–Therapia |
| 9 | ARABIAN NIGHT | 3 8–4 | C. Smirke. b.c. by Persian Gulf–Faerie Lore |
| 10 | BARTON STREET | 3 8–4 | J. Sime. br.c. by Watling Street–Scarborough Lily |
| 11 | CHATSWORTH | 4 9–4 | F. Barlow. b.c. by Chanteur II–Netherton Maid |
| 12 | RASHLEIGH | 3 8–4 | W. Snaith. br.c. by Precipitation–Eastags |
| 13 | JANITOR (FR) (b) | 4 9–4 | J. Doyasbere. br.c. by Pharis II–Orlamonde |
| 14 | ALTANA | 3 8–1 | E. Mercer. b.f. by Arbar–Palencia |
| 15 | PREMONITION | 4 9–4 | W. Carr. b.c. by Precipitation–Trial Ground |
| 16 | CORONATION SCOT | 3 8–4 | D. Smith. b.c. by Naucide–Silver Blue |
| 17 | GOLDEN GOD | 3 8–4 | W. Rickaby. gr.c. by Migoli–Gilded Bee |

17 Ran

Going – Dead

Distances: ¾,2,4,2,½

Time: 2:44.00

S.P. 9–2 AUREOLE, 5–1 BOTTICELLI, 7–1 ARABIAN NIGHT, 9–1 PREMONITION, 10–1 JANITOR, 100–7 CHAMIER, VAMOS, BARTON STREET, 100–6 ALTANA, 18–1 ELOPEMENT, 20–1 DARIUS, RASHLEIGH, 33–1 OTHERS

Winner trained by C. Boyd-Rochfort at Newmarket: owned by Her Majesty the Queen: bred by King George VI

Timeform rating of winner 132

# 1955

In 1955 M. Pierre Wertheimer's VIMY became the first French-trained winner of the King George.

By Wild Risk, dual winner of the French Champion Hurdle, out of Mimi, VIMY made only six racecourse appearances during his two years in training with Chantilly-based trainer Alec Head. Those who saw VIMY finish last of twenty-two runners on his two-year-old debut at Maisons-Laffitte, probably dismissed the colt as being of little account. One would have needed a fully functional crystal ball to have had the inspiration to label VIMY a future middle-distance champion of Europe.

One week after his ignoble debut, VIMY contested the Prix de l'Ormay at Longchamp. In scrambling home by a short head from a mediocre collection of opponents, Head's colt hardly set the racing world alight and so, having won one of his two races as a juvenile, VIMY was rated twenty-three pounds below the top weight Beau Prince II in the French Free Handicap.

Reappearing in the Prix Lagrange over ten furlongs at Maisons-Laffitte, VIMY turned in a performance at least twelve pounds above anything he had achieved the previous season. Running over a distance of ground for the first time, VIMY came with a powerful late run to share the spoils with the useful Nordic. Stepping up to eleven furlongs in the Prix Noailles at Longchamp, VIMY handed out a four-length beating to Zinosca.

Clearly the colt was improving with every race, and Head decided to grasp the nettle by taking on the top French three-year-old colts in the Prix du Jockey-Club. Although inconvenienced by the soft going, VIMY ran a marvellous race at Chantilly, only giving best to Rapace in the very last stride. After the race, connections announced that VIMY would take on the best horses in Europe in the King George.

VIMY attracted plenty of support at Ascot, including one individual bet of £20,000 to £2,000, but he was sent off only fourth favourite at 10–1, behind Phil Drake, Acropolis, and Hugh Lupus. The François Mathet-trained Phil Drake dominated the market, backed down from 5–4 to his starting price of 8–11. A tall, rangy colt by Admiral Drake, Phil Drake did not race at two. After finishing second on his debut at Longchamp, he won the Prix la Rochette over the same course by an impressive four lengths. Sent to contest the Epsom Derby, Madame Volterra's colt came with a wet sail inside the final furlong to win the Blue Riband by a length and a half from Panaslipper. In his final race before Ascot, Phil Drake broke the Longchamp one mile, seven furlongs course record by two seconds, when coasting home in the Grand Prix de Paris.

The other two French challengers, Elu and Cordova II, were very much second division material, and attracted little interest at 33–1.

The main English challenge was expected to come from Cecil Boyd-Rochfort's Acropolis, third behind Phil Drake and Panaslipper in the Derby and from the four-year-old Darius, third to Aureole in the 1954 King George and recent winner of the Eclipse Stakes. The Irish sent a three-strong challenge consisting of Arctic Time, Hugh Lupus, and Zarathustra. Although Arctic Time was likely to find himself outclassed in such exalted company, Irish Two Thousand Guineas winner Hugh Lupus, and Zarathustra, successful in both the 1954 Irish Derby and Irish St Leger, were expected to run well.

It was noticeable during the parade that Phil Drake had run up light since his last run, and he went down to the start rather scratchily. Doug Smith on Acropolis was under instruction to ensure that the race was run at a strong pace. He was anxious to avoid the race developing into a sprint up the short Ascot straight, where, without that vital turn of foot, his mount would be at a distinct disadvantage. In the event, Smith's tactics almost paid off. Blazing along in front, Acropolis turned into the home straight with a two-length advantage over Arctic Time. Jockey Poincelet, who had kept VIMY tight against the rails throughout, found himself boxed in behind Arctic Time and Hugh Lupus as the field straightened up for home. Fortunately for the Frenchman, a gap appeared just inside the two furlong marker, and he was able to squeeze his mount through into a challenging position.

Inside the last two hundred yards the race developed into a titanic duel between Acropolis and VIMY, the pair drawing right away from their rivals. With Poincelet riding like a man possessed, the French colt headed Acropolis inside the distance. Smith's mount was far from finished, however, and bravely clawed his way back into the reckoning. The result was in doubt right up to the line. Both horses flashed past the post together, but the blue and white Wertheimer colours just held the advantage by a head. Lester Piggott's mount Elopement ran on to be third, three lengths behind the two principals, with the rest of the field bunched up behind.

VIMY, last of twenty-two in his first race, was duly admitted into the élite of the racing world thanks to his victory in the King George. A plan by connections to send the colt to Doncaster for the St Leger had to be aborted when he was found to be jarred-up on returning from Ascot.

VIMY did not race again after Ascot. After a period at the Irish National Stud, he was exported to Japan in 1964. Although he failed to sire any champions himself, VIMY mares have been responsible for Busted, Linden Tree, and High Top.

# 1955

## KING GEORGE VI AND QUEEN ELIZABETH STAKES
£23,430    1m 4f

July 16, 1955

| 1 VIMY (FR) | 3 8–4 | R. Poincelet. b.c. by Wild Risk–Mimi |
|---|---|---|
| 2 ACROPOLIS | 3 8–4 | D. Smith. ch.c. by Donatello II–Aurora |
| 3 ELOPEMENT | 4 9–4 | L. Piggott. ch.c. by Rockefella–Daring Miss |
| 4 ARCTIC TIME | 3 8–4 | J. Eddery. br.c. by Arctic Star–Dancing Time |
| 5 HUGH LUPUS | 3 8–4 | W. Johnstone. b.c. by Djebel–Sakountala |
| 6 PHIL DRAKE | 3 8–4 | F. Palmer. b.c. by Admiral Drake–Philippa |
| 7 ZARATHUSTRA | 4 9–4 | P. Powell. jun.bl.c. by Persian Gulf–Salvia |
| 8 ELU (FR) | 6 9–4 | C. Lalanne. b.h. by Eble–Lucques |
| 9 DARIUS | 4 9–4 | E. Smith. b.c. by Dante–Yasna |
| 10 CORDOVA II (FR) | 4 9–1 | S. Boullenger. b.f. by Djebel–Caravelle |

10 Ran

Going – Firm

Distances: hd,3,hd,hd,1

Time: 2:33.76

S.P. 8–11 PHIL DRAKE, 11–12 ACROPOLIS, 9–1 HUGH LUPUS, 10–1 VIMY, 12–1 DARIUS, 25–1 ELOPEMENT, 33–1 OTHERS

Winner trained by Alec Head in France: owned by M. P. Wertheimer: bred by owner

Timeform rating of winner 132

# 1956

O n July 21st, 1956, while politicians took the stage for the prologue to the impending Suez Crisis, the eyes of the racing world were sharply focused on Ascot racecourse, the scene of a rather different battle of wits. The brilliant Italian champion RIBOT, unbeaten in thirteen races, was about to contest the King George. Thousands flocked to catch a glimpse of the Latin superstar on his first appearance on a British racecourse. RIBOT did not let his supporters down. He won the victory, but he was made to fight hard for his laurels.

Bred by the legendary Federico Tesio, the man responsible for the 1938 champion Nearco, RIBOT was named after the nineteenth-century French artist Theodule-Augustin Ribot. Although he was a product of the Marchese Incisa della Rochetta's Razza Dormello, a picturesque stud on the shores of Lake Maggiore, RIBOT was actually foaled at the English National Stud where his dam Romanella was making a second visit to the stallion Tenerani. RIBOT came from solid stock. Tenerani was a dual Classic winner in Italy, with victories in the Derby and St Leger to his credit, while Romanella had been a smart two-year-old, winning five races including the prestigious Criterium Nazionale.

As a yearling RIBOT was so small that the stable lads labelled him "Il Piccolo" – the little one. Because of his stature, RIBOT was not entered for the early-closing Italian Classic races, and so one of the greatest racehorses of the twentieth century was denied the chance to compete for Classic glory.

RIBOT went into training with Ugo Penco, who took over the Marchese's horses on the death of Tesio in May 1954. He ran three times during his first season, winning over five furlongs, six furlongs and seven and a half furlongs at the San Siro track in Milan. At the close of the 1954 season he topped the Italian Two-Year-Old Free Handicap.

RIBOT began the 1955 season with an emphatic win in the Premio Pisa. Penco then sent his colt to contest the Premio Emanuele Filberto at Milan. Although RIBOT retained his unbeaten record, beating the useful Gail by ten lengths, he finished so lame that it took his rider, Enrico Camici, all of five minutes to guide him into the winner's enclosure. Many feared that the rock hard going had prematurely ended the colt's promising career. After a period of convalescence, however, RIBOT was fully recovered from his injury and he returned to Milan to record his sixth consecutive victory. Six weeks later he was back again, romping home by ten lengths in the Premio Besnate. Penco then decided to cast his net wider. RIBOT was sent to Longchamp to take on the best horses in Europe in the Prix de l'Arc de Triomphe. The Italian champion captured the hearts of the Parisians with a spectacular three-length success over Beau Prince, thus staking his claim to being the best middle-distance performer in Europe.

Penco was not one to allow his horses to rest on their laurels, and so two weeks after his Arc triumph, RIBOT was back in action, slamming a field of moderate opponents by fifteen lengths in the Premio del Jockey Club at San Siro. By his fourth year, "Il Piccolo" had become "Il Grande", having grown to be almost sixteen hands. Although still far from handsome, RIBOT radiated charisma, and attracted admiring glances each time he appeared in public.

RIBOT won four races at Milan in the early part of 1956, humiliating his rivals by an aggregate of thirty-two lengths. By now a national hero he was set the task of becoming the first Italian-trained winner of the King George. Unbeaten in thirteen consecutive races and the undisputed champion of Europe, defeat at Ascot appeared unthinkable. In the event, however, the 2–5 favourite found himself involved in the hardest race of his glittering career.

The challenger who almost succeeded in piercing RIBOT's armour, was the Queen's High Veldt. Trained by Cecil Boyd-Rochfort, he was by Hyperion, sire of the 1954 winner Aureole. A rather highly strung individual, High Veldt had won both the Two Thousand Guineas Trial Stakes at Kempton, and the Thirsk Classic Trial earlier in the season. Strictly on paper, the Queen's colt had no chance of beating the favourite, but somebody obviously forgot to show him the relevant pages in the form book.

The nine-runner field eventually got under way at the second attempt, the Belgian challenger Todrai having broken the tapes on the first line-up. High Veldt was the first to show, but was steadied by Carr after about half a furlong. At the halfway stage, Daemon led the field from Todrai and RIBOT. Turning out of Swinley Bottom, Todrai hit the front, with RIBOT, High Veldt, and Chantelsey bunched in behind. As the leaders rounded the home turn, a gasp went up from the grandstand as the crowd realised that the Italian horse, unhappy on the soft ground, was being ridden along by Camici. As High Veldt moved up to RIBOT's quarters, home supporters began to cheer on the English challenger. The two horses were neck and neck at the two furlong pole.

Suddenly, however, the whole complexion of the race changed. As RIBOT hit the better ground inside the last furlong and a half, he changed gear, and lengthening his stride, he sprinted clear of High Veldt. At the line he had five lengths to spare over the gallant royal representative. RIBOT had survived the biggest test of his career, and retained his unbeaten record. He remains the only Italian-trained winner of the King George.

After Ascot, RIBOT won the Premio del Piazzale, beating the Italian Two Thousand Guineas winner Magabit by eight lengths. His swan song came at Longchamp, where he slammed the Irish Derby winner Talgo by six lengths to record his second Arc victory.

There is something magical about an unbeaten horse. RIBOT retired with his record intact, the winner of all sixteen of his races. He stood at Lord Derby's Woodland Stud in Newmarket for one season, before returning to his native Italy. RIBOT was finally transferred to Kentucky, where, despite growing intractability, he proved a stallion of immense influence. The leading sire in England in 1963, 1967 and 1968, RIBOT produced an impressive list of Group and Stakes race winners on both sides of the Atlantic—Ragusa, Tom Rolfe, Graustark, Arts and Letters, Ribocco and Ribero are just a selection of his illustrious offspring.

RIBOT died in 1972.

# 1956

## KING GEORGE VI AND QUEEN ELIZABETH STAKES

£23,727 10s    1m 4f

July 21, 1956

| 1 RIBOT (ITY) | 4 9–4 | E. Camici. ch.c. by Tenerani–Romanella |
|---|---|---|
| 2 HIGH VELDT | 3 8–4 | W. Carr. ch.c. by Hyperion–Open Country |
| 3 TODRAI (BEL) | 3 8–4 | V. Vandendriesche. ch.c. by Le Destroyer–Toute Bonne |
| 4 KURUN (FR) | 4 9–4 | C. Smirke. ch.c. by Whirlaway–Asmena |
| 5 ROISTAR | 3 8–4 | J. Eddery. b.c. by Arctic Star–Roisin |
| 6 CASH AND COURAGE | 3 8–4 | E. Smith. b.c. by Rockefella–Daring Miss |
| 7 CHANTELSEY | 3 8–4 | E. Britt. ch.c. by Pardal–Chantage |
| 8 DAEMON | 4 9–4 | G. Lewis. b.c. by Niccolo Dell'Arca–Kyanos |
| 9 PATRAS (FR) | 3 8–4 | F. Palmer. ch.c. by Goyama–Madame Patrol |

9 Ran

Going – Soft

Distances: 5,2,½,8,1½

Time: 2:40.24

S.P. 2–5 RIBOT, 10–1 CHANTELSEY, 12–1 ROISTAR, 100–7 HIGH VELDT, KURUN, 25–1 CASH AND COURAGE, 33–1 OTHERS

Winner trained by Ugo Penco in Italy: owned by Marchese Incisa della Rochetta: bred by Razza Dormello, in Italy

Timeform rating of winner 142

# 1957

The 1957 King George proved to be a benefit race for the French, with Gallic raiders filling the first four places. The field was, however, one of the weakest in the history of the race, and the winner, MONTAVAL, has sound claims to being the worst ever winner of the Ascot showpiece.

The race was devalued as a championship event by the absence of the Two Thousand Guineas and Derby winner, Crepello. Noel Murless's colt had been an intended runner until the morning of the race, and had frightened off all serious opposition. Unfortunately, terrific overnight thunderstorms resulted in boglike conditions, with going officially described as "dead". Crepello was withdrawn at the eleventh hour, leaving twelve inferior animals to fight for the £23,090 first prize.

Ralph Strassburger's MONTAVAL was a rather common-looking bay colt by Norseman. His record prior to Ascot made unimpressive reading. Successful in one minor race from five attempts as a two-year-old, he began his second season with a dismal display in the Prix Lagrange at Maisons-Laffitte where he trailed in last of the six runners. After taking second place in the Prix Daru, MONTAVAL astonished the world by almost winning a sub-standard Epsom Derby. Sent off a 40–1 chance, he just failed to hold his compatriot, Lavandin, by a neck.

Unfortunately, MONTAVAL reverted to his mediocre former self after Epsom. In five subsequent races he managed just a single victory, and even that came against extremely weak opposition, in the Prix Gontaut-Biron at Deauville. MONTAVAL continued his pursuit of adequacy as a four-year-old, in the Prix Ganay. There was scant sign of improvement, and the colt trailed home unplaced behind Tanerko.

After two minor victories at Longchamp, MONTAVAL crossed the Channel to contest the Eclipse Stakes. Although he never threatened to win the race, he collected third prize behind Arctic Explorer and Pirate King. More in hope than confidence, connections decided to let MONTAVAL take his chance in the King George, reasoning that somebody had to finish second to Crepello! Even with the Derby winner's enforced absence, MONTAVAL's chances of landing the prize were realistically rated at 20–1.

To be fair to him, there was a case to be made against most of the twelve runners. Alec Head's Al Mabsoot was a temperamental sort who needed covering up, a manoeuvre not easily executed on a hard puller: Fric, winner of the Coronation Cup and the Hardwicke Stakes, was probably the best horse in the field, but he needed a sound surface to show his best form: Jack Ketch, the Irish Two Thousand Guineas winner was unproven over twelve furlongs, while Herbert Blagrave's China Rock, and the Italian challenger, Tissot, undoubtedly needed further. With the Queen's High Veldt looking only a shadow of the horse who had given the mighty Ribot such a fright twelve months earlier, and the remainder of the field appearing second-raters, it was difficult to nominate a winner.

With the ground so testing, it was inevitable that the pace would be slow. The early leaders, Tissot and Fric, set a moderate gallop, and the race developed into a sprint up the marshy straight. With two furlongs to run, the French raiders Al Mabsoot and MONTAVAL had the finish to themselves, the rest of the field already floundering behind. At the furlong pole MONTAVAL appeared to have the upper hand. Slowly but surely however, Massard inched his mount up to join the leader, the pair matching strides with 150 yards to go.

A hundred yards out Al Mabsoot snatched the advantage and looked certain to win. Now it was the turn of the older horse to fight back. Gaining with every stride, MONTAVAL gradually wore down his rival, inch by inch. The pair flashed past the post together in one of the closest finishes in the history of the King George. The verdict went to MONTAVAL by the narrowest margin. The principals finished two lengths clear of Tribord who ran on inside the final furlong to take minor honours.

MONTAVAL's final racecourse appearance came in the Washington

International at Laurel Park where he finished a disappointing seventh of eight.

Purchased by the Earl of Harrington, MONTAVAL began his stallion career in Ireland, prior to being exported to Japan in 1961.

# 1957

## KING GEORGE VI AND QUEEN ELIZABETH STAKES

£23,090    1m 4f

July 20, 1957

| 1 MONTAVAL (FR) | 4 9–7 | F. Palmer. b.c. by Norseman–Ballynash |
|---|---|---|
| 2 AL MABSOOT (FR) | 3 8–7 | J. Massard. b.c. by Mat de Cocagne–Rose O'Lynn |
| 3 TRIBORD (FR) | 6 9–7 | J. Fabre. b.h. by Bozzetto–Troie |
| 4 SAINT RAPHAEL (FR) | 4 9–7 | F. Bonni. ch.c. by Foxlight–Santa Paula |
| 5 TALGO | 4 9–7 | E. Mercer. b.c. by Krakatao–Miss France |
| 6 FRIC | 5 9–7 | J. Deforge. br.h. by Vandale–Fripe |
| 7 JACK KETCH | 3 8–7 | C. Smirke. br.c. by Abadan–Law |
| 8 TODRAI (BEL) | 4 9–7 | C. Nagy, b.c. by Le Destroyer–Toute Bonne |
| 9 OROSO (FR) | 4 9–7 | L. Flavien. br.c. by Tifinar–Eos |
| 10 TISSOT (ITY) | 4 9–7 | E. Camici. b.c. by Tenerani–Tiepoletta II |
| 11 CHINA ROCK | 4 9–7 | F. Durr. ch.c. by Rockefella–May Wong |
| 12 HIGH VELDT | 4 9–7 | W. Carr. ch.c. by Hyperion–Open Country |

12 Ran

Going – Dead

Distances: sht hd,2,4,6,5

Time: 2:41.02

S.P. 5–2 TISSOT, 9–1 TALGO, 10–1 CHINA ROCK, TODRAI, FRIC, 100–9 JACK KETCH, 100–8 OROSO, 100–7 TRIBORD, AL MABSOOT, 20–1 MONTAVAL, 20–1 OTHERS

Winner trained by G. Bridgland in France: owned by Mr R. Strassburger: bred by owner

Timeform rating of winner 129

# 1958

The late fifties were crucial years in the career of Vincent O'Brien. The Tipperary trainer had achieved spectacular success under National Hunt rules with three Grand Nationals, four Cheltenham Gold Cups and three Champion Hurdles to his credit. Ambitious to make his mark in the more lucrative sphere of Flat racing, he set about the task of finding owners who had the financial resources to support such a transition. In the coming years, O'Brien would train horses for some of the richest men in the world – owners like Charles Engelhard and Stavros Niarchos – but initially it was the American millionaire John McShain's chestnut colt BALLYMOSS who pushed O'Brien into the Classic spotlight.

Purchased by O'Brien on behalf of McShain for 4,500 guineas at the 1955 Tattersalls' September Sales, BALLYMOSS was the first in a long line of Classic winners acquired by the Irishman at public auction. Initially, however, the man now acknowledged as perhaps the greatest living judge of bloodstock in the world, appeared to have overestimated the potential of the son of Mossborough.

BALLYMOSS contested four races as a two-year-old, winning just one of them. After being unplaced on his debut at the Curragh, he improved to take second place behind Bell Bird at Mallow. BALLYMOSS finally lost his maiden tag over seven furlongs at Leopardstown where he had two lengths to spare over El Mizah. After filling the runner-up spot on his final outing of 1956, BALLYMOSS was allotted eight stone, eleven pounds in the Irish Free Handicap, seventeen pounds behind the top-rated Skindles Hotel. Although the chestnut had only one victory to his name, O'Brien retained his confidence in the colt, describing him in a letter to his American owner as having, "definite possibilities as a Classic horse".

Many sons of Mossborough had proved to be rather colty. BALLY-

MOSS was no exception and during his second season he became quite difficult. Fortunately O'Brien was able to manage the chestnut without resorting to the surgeon's knife.

After finishing in the ruck in the Madrid Free Handicap at the Curragh on his seasonal reappearance, BALLYMOSS earned a place in the Derby line-up with a neck victory in the twelve furlong Trigo Stakes at Leopardstown. The colt clearly appreciated running over a distance of ground, and put up a tremendous performance at Epsom, only giving second best to the Lester Piggott-ridden Crepello.

With Crepello still in his box at Newmarket, BALLYMOSS scored his first Classic success in the Irish Derby. Never off the bit, he crushed Hindu Festival by an effortless four lengths, a winning margin which could easily have been doubled.

BALLYMOSS next contested the Great Voltigeur Stakes at York. On going officially described as "dead", the Irish Derby winner was surprisingly beaten four lengths by the northern-trained Brioche. Undeterred, O'Brien aimed his stable star at the oldest Classic, the St Leger. In beating Court Harwell by a length, BALLYMOSS became the first ever Irish-trained winner of the race.

Now a dual Classic winner, BALLYMOSS crossed the Irish Sea to contest the Champion Stakes at Newmarket. Over a distance which was almost certainly on the short side, he ran a lifeless race to finish sixth, behind Rose Royale II. It later transpired that the colt had injured himself when lashing out at the rails in the parade ring prior to the race.

After his winter rest, BALLYMOSS reappeared in the Ormonde Stakes at Chester. Looking on the burly side, he was beaten by one and a half lengths by Doutelle, but was not subjected to a hard race once his chance had gone.

A much fitter BALLYMOSS started even money favourite for the Coronation Cup, and had little difficulty in accounting for the useful Fric by two lengths. A six-length victory against second-rate opposition in the Eclipse Stakes at Sandown, ensured that the chestnut would start favourite for the King George – if he ran. Normally there would have been no question of his participation, but this season O'Brien and McShain held an extremely strong hand in the top middle-distance races with the talented mare Gladness, also a resident at Ballydoyle. The decision was left to the Almighty. If the going was soft, Gladness would run but if the rains stayed away, the colt would represent the stable. The going was good and BALLYMOSS ran.

He faced seven rivals at Ascot, two of which had the form to win. His main market rival was the three-year-old Hard Ridden, Charlie Smirke's mount, with two Classics under his belt – the Irish Two Thousand Guineas and the Epsom Derby. Despite beating a sub-standard field in the Blue Riband, he attracted plenty of support at 2–1. Almeria, another rival, trained at Newmarket by Cecil Boyd-Rochfort, was an exceptionally attractive filly who had won the Ribblesdale Stakes, the Yorkshire Oaks and the Park Hill Stakes in 1957. Although twelve furlongs was a shade on the sharp side for her, connections were more than hopeful of landing the £23,642 10s first prize.

The filly was the first out of the gates, setting a moderate pace in the hands of Harry Carr. Breasley was content to hold up BALLYMOSS in the rear while his rivals disputed the lead. After a mile only two horses were still on the bit – Almeria and BALLYMOSS. In behind, Hard Ridden was living up to his name and making little progress.

Breasley timed his run to perfection, coming to challenge Almeria at the two furlong marker. Although Carr conjured up a renewed effort from his filly, the partnership were fighting a losing battle, BALLYMOSS sweeping into the lead in effortless fashion. The race was over in a matter of strides, the Irish challenger putting daylight between himself and his rivals. At the post BALLYMOSS was three lengths clear of Almeria, with Doutelle back in third.

The King George hero went on to crown a marvellous season by winning the Prix de l'Arc de Triomphe in tremendous fashion, beating Fric by two easy lengths. Then having proved himself the best horse in Europe, BALLYMOSS crossed the Atlantic to take on the Americans in the Washington International at Laurel Park. In the event, he was unable to handle the tight track, and could only finish third to Tudor Era and Sailor's Guide. He was subsequently promoted to second after the winner had been disqualified for bumping the runner-up.

A game and genuine performer, who fully justified his trainer's optimism, BALLYMOSS retired to the Banstead Manor Stud, the winner of £107,165 in prize money. While O'Brien went on to further glory, BALLYMOSS proved somewhat disappointing as a stallion, although he did sire the Derby and King George winner Royal Palace.

# 1958

## KING GEORGE VI AND QUEEN ELIZABETH STAKES

£23,642 10s      1 m 4f

July 19, 1958

| 1 BALLYMOSS | 4 9–7 | A. Breasley. ch.c. by Mossborough–Indian Call |
|---|---|---|
| 2 ALMERIA | 4 9–4 | W. Carr. ch.f. by Alycidon–Auila |
| 3 DOUTELLE | 4 9–7 | J. Mercer. ch.c. by Prince Chevalier–Above Board |
| 4 AL MABSOOT (FR) | 4 9–7 | R. Poincelet. b.c. by Mat de Cocagne–Rose O'Lynn |
| 5 CHINA ROCK | 5 9–7 | D. Purtell. ch.h. by Rockefella–May Wong |
| 6 HARD RIDDEN | 3 8–7 | C. Smirke. b.c. by Hard Source–Toute Belle II |
| 7 THILA (FR) | 4 9–4 | G. Lequeux. bl.f. by Magnat–Thilde |
| 8 BRIOCHE | 4 9–7 | E. Britt. b.c. by Tantième–Eudemis |

8 Ran

Going – Good

Distances: 3,¾,¾,nk,½

Time: 2:36.33

S.P. 7–4 BALLYMOSS, 2–1 HARD RIDDEN, 9–1 ALMERIA, 100–9 THILA, 100–8 BRIOCHE, 100–7 DOUTELLE, AL MABSOOT, 50–1 CHINA ROCK

Winner trained by M. V. O'Brien at Cashel, Co Tipperary: owned by Mr J. McShain: bred by Mr R. Ball in Ireland

Timeform rating of winner 136

# 1959

Cecil Boyd-Rochfort's Freemason Lodge stables housed two outstanding individuals in 1959 – Parthia, the Epsom Derby winner, and a rather plain looking four-year-old colt called ALCIDE.

Owned by Jockey Club member Sir Humphrey de Trafford, ALCIDE had been a tiny creature as a yearling. A dark bay with black points, he was bred for stamina, being by the Ascot Gold Cup winner Alycidon out of the stoutly bred mare Chenille.

As a two-year-old, ALCIDE was bone idle and would sulk his way onto the gallops rather like Shakespeare's "whining schoolboy . . . creeping like snail unwillingly to school". To the surprise of his connections and the bewilderment of breeding experts, however, the reluctant, stoutly bred ALCIDE won the seven furlong Horris Hill Stakes on his second and final appearance as a juvenile.

Boyd-Rochfort's colt reappeared in the Royal Stakes at Sandown where he narrowly failed to concede seven pounds to the Lester Piggott-ridden Snow Cat. After victories in the Chester Vase and the Lingfield Derby trial, ALCIDE became a victim of his own success. The new Derby favourite was found lying in his box in considerable pain. He had been viciously attacked with a blunt instrument and had suffered a broken rib and extensive bruising. His mystery assailants had achieved their aim—ALCIDE never made it to Epsom.

Three months after this incident, Sir Humphrey de Trafford's colt returned in triumph with a scintillating fifteen-length victory in the Great Voltigeur Stakes at York. He was now a hot favourite for the St Leger and the subject of intense security. St Leger day dawned, and ALCIDE arrived at Doncaster unmolested to win the final Classic by eight lengths without coming off the bit. He was improving with every race, so connections decided to keep him in training as a four-year-old, with the Ascot Gold Cup as his principal target.

As in the past, ALCIDE needed a race to achieve peak fitness, and connections were not too concerned when he was beaten by the minimum distance in the Jockey Club Cup on his first outing of 1959. The son of Alycidon derived considerable benefit from the race and went on to land the Victor Wild Stakes at Kempton in the fastest time recorded over the course and distance for twenty-five years.

After easily winning the Winston Churchill Stakes at Hurst Park, ALCIDE was made ante-post favourite for the Ascot Gold Cup since the two and a half-mile trip looked ready-made for Boyd-Rochfort's colt. Two weeks before Royal Ascot, ALCIDE jarred a joint on the Heath, an injury which interrupted his meticulously planned big race preparation. But despite missing a number of vital gallops, he ran a tremendous race in the Gold Cup, going under by the shortest of short heads to the French raider Wallaby II.

After the Gold Cup, connections announced that ALCIDE would revert to a mile and a half in the King George. Although many pundits doubted the wisdom of taking on the best middle-distance horses with a proven stayer, jockey Harry Carr was so confident that he would win, he ordered the traditional victory champagne prior to the race!

Although his Ascot Gold Cup conqueror Wallaby II was in the line-up, ALCIDE was expected to gain his revenge on the French horse. The main dangers appeared to be the Irish mare Gladness, and the northern hope Cantelo. Connections of Gladness were hoping to land a second successive King George after their 1958 triumph with Ballymoss. The Vincent O'Brien-trained six-year-old was sent off the 9–2 second favourite, largely on the strength of her previous season's form which saw her an impressive winner of the Ascot Gold Cup. Charles Elsey's three-year-old filly Cantelo was one of the best horses trained in the north for many a year. The winner of all six of her races prior to contesting the Oaks, she was far from disgraced at Epsom, where she beat all but the great Petite Etoile. In her only other race prior to the King George, she ran out a one and a half length winner of the Ribblesdale Stakes.

Under a clear blue Berkshire sky, the eleven runners were despatched at the first attempt. Chief III, trained at Chantilly by Alec Head, was the first from the gate, closely followed by Orsini and

[ 39 ]

Cantelo. The French horse still held the lead turning into the straight, but the serious contenders were about to make their challenges from the rear. ALCIDE had only two horses behind him with three furlongs to run, but he was going easily under Harry Carr. Unfortunately for the favourite's supporters, Gladness was also cruising as the field levelled up for home.

It was the Irish-trained mare who made the first move, taking the lead from the weakening Chief III at the two furlong marker. With Cantelo also under pressure, and the rest of the field strung out behind, it was left to ALCIDE to save the day for the home team. Making steady progress on the outside of the field, Carr brought his mount with an irresistible challenge taking him past seven of his rivals in the space of a furlong. Inside the distance ALCIDE snatched the lead from Gladness, and quickly settled the issue with a powerful spurt which saw him home by a couple of lengths. In a truly cosmopolitan finish, the French horse Balbo, a 33–1 shot, got up close home to snatch third place from Cantelo.

After the race, Carr, who had fought a running battle against the scales throughout his career, was rushed to hospital suffering from kidney malfunction, the result of sustained wasting in the week leading up to the race. After two weeks of care he was able to enjoy that champagne he had so confidently requested.

As for ALCIDE, he was retired to stud after the King George. A truly versatile performer who won races at distances between seven furlongs and two miles, he never really set the world alight as a stallion and many of his produce turned out to be rather highly strung. He died in 1973.

## 1959

### KING GEORGE VI AND QUEEN ELIZABETH STAKES

£23,642 10s    1m 4f

July 18, 1959

| | | |
|---|---|---|
| 1 ALCIDE | 4 9–7 | W. Carr. b.c. by Alycidon–Chenille |
| 2 GLADNESS | 6 9–4 | G. Bougoure. b.m. by Sayajirao–Bright Lady |
| 3 BALBO (FR) | 5 9–7 | J. Boullenger. ch.h. by Apple Pie–Blue Bottle |
| 4 CANTELO | 3 8–4 | E. Hide. b.f. by Chanteur II–Rustic Bridge |
| 5 ORSINI (GER) | 5 9–7 | A. Klimschasen. br.h. by Ticino–Oranien |
| 6 PINDARI | 3 8–7 | L. Piggott. br.c. by Pinza–Sun Chariot |
| 7 CHIEF III (FR) | 6 9–7 | G. Lequeux. b.h. by Nearco–Nikellora |
| 8 AMOURROU | 3 8–7 | J. Lindley. ch.c. by Worden II–Army Flirt |
| 9 MIRNAYA | 3 8–4 | D. Smith. b.f. by Nearco–Solar System |
| 10 AL MABSOOT (FR) | 5 9–7 | G. Moore. b.h. by Mat de Cocagne–Rose O'Lynn |
| 11 WALLABY II (FR) | 4 9–7 | F. Palmer. b.c. by Fast Fox–Wagging Tail |

11 Ran

Going – Good

Distances: 2,¾,3,nk,2

Time: 2:31.39

S.P. 2–1 ALCIDE, 9–2 GLADNESS, 5–1 WALLABY II, 6–1 CANTELO, 8–1 PINDARI, 9–1 MIRNAYA, 22–1 AL MABSOOT, 25–1 AMOURROU, 33–1 OTHERS

Winner trained by Cecil Boyd-Rochfort at Newmarket: owned by Sir Humphrey de Trafford: bred by owner

Timeform rating of winner 136

# 1960

The 1960 King George resulted in the defeat of one of the most brilliant fillies of modern times. Any student of the Turf who witnessed the race will still admit to utter astonishment at its outcome for time has not lessened the impact of such a reversal. Petite Etoile, the darling of Newmarket, the heroine of nine consecutive races prior to Ascot, was beaten by a horse considered by many to be inferior to her by pounds. How could such a dramatic upset have happened? Where were the clues which had to be assembled before the mystery could be solved?

After winning two of her four races as a two-year-old, Petite Etoile set the racing world alight in 1959 with scintillating victories in the Free Handicap, the Thousand Guineas, Oaks, Sussex Stakes, Yorkshire Oaks and the Champion Stakes.

The daughter of Petition continued her winning ways as a four-year-old with clear-cut victories in the Victor Wild Stakes at Kempton and in the Coronation Cup, beating the 1959 Derby winner Parthia by an effortless one and a half lengths. The King George seemed at the mercy of the flying grey.

June proved to be a wicked month for Petite Etoile and her connections. Owner Prince Aly Khan was killed in a car crash and so the filly became the property of his son Karim. Then she developed a cough which threatened her participation in the King George. Trainer Noel Murless, a magician with fillies, nursed her back to fitness with a combination of skill and patience, producing her in magnificent condition on King George day, apparently with little to fear from any of her seven opponents.

AGGRESSOR, rejected as a yearling by Cecil Boyd-Rochfort in the belief that he lacked the scope to make a top-class performer, won three of his six starts as a two-year-old. At three the son of Combat held no classic engagements but proved himself to be of classic standard by beating the subsequent Guineas winner Pall Mall in the Two Thousand Guineas Trial Stakes at Kempton Park. AGGRESSOR continued to improve and won the Coronation Stakes and the Cumberland Lodge Stakes as a four-year-old. Enterprisingly kept in training with the 1960 King George in mind, the bay picked up both the John Porter Stakes and the Hardwicke Stakes prior to Ascot. Despite this consistent record, few "experts" gave AGGRESSOR much chance of beating Petite Etoile. Trainer John Gosden and jockey Jimmy Lindley, however, were more than hopeful of bustling up the favourite.

Parthia, the 1959 Derby winner, was a lazy type. After winning the Jockey Club Cup at Newmarket on his seasonal reappearance, Boyd-Rochfort's horse had a simple task to win the Paradise Stakes at Hurst Park. On his next outing Parthia was soundly beaten by Petite Etoile in the Coronation Cup. The Derby winner's star lost even more of its lustre with a comprehensive defeat by AGGRESSOR in the Hardwicke Stakes at Royal Ascot. Connections were, however, hopeful that at level weights (Parthia had given AGGRESSOR six pounds in the Hardwicke), the son of Persian Gulf might turn the tables on his rival in the King George. Of the remaining runners only the Paddy Prendergast-trained Kythnos had any realistic hope of reaching the frame. After winning the Irish Two Thousand Guineas the colt ran a creditable third to St Paddy in the Epsom Derby.

In addition to her seven equine opponents, Petite Etoile also had to contend with softer ground than she had ever encountered. Although the going was officially described as good, heavy overnight rain had deadened the ground considerably. Her stamina was unproved on anything other than top-of-the-ground conditions.

From the break, the Italian-trained De Voos went into a four-length lead with Parthia, Flores III, Sunny Court, and AGGRESSOR closely bunched in behind. Piggott held up Petite Etoile at the rear of the field. Approaching the turn into the straight, Parthia began to lose his place as Flores III took over the lead from De Voos. At this stage Piggott made his move on Petite Etoile only to be bumped by the Breasley-ridden Sunny Court. As AGGRESSOR hit the front two furlongs out, Piggott found himself trapped behind a wall of horses. Switched to the wide outside, Petite Etoile began to make rapid headway inside the final furlong, but AGGRESSOR had stolen first run and held on to win by half a length with Kythnos a further four lengths back in third.

After the race Piggott was severely criticised by the racing press for his apparent overconfidence. Murless, however, refused to blame his jockey. The Newmarket trainer argued that Petite Etoile had always been difficult to train due to her idiosyncratic nature and volatile temperament. He also believed that with speed on both sides of her pedigree, the grey did not really stay one and a half miles on testing going and so had to be held up until the last possible moment.

So perhaps it was a combination of several factors that brought about the shock defeat of Petite Etoile. It was likely that she was still suffering from the after-effects of the cough; she possibly failed to stay the trip on the kind of dead ground she had never experienced; Piggott's exaggerated waiting tactics had been unsuited to the short Ascot straight and she had met bad luck in running. Most obvious of all, it did seem possible that the winner, AGGRESSOR, had previously been seriously underrated.

After the King George there were plans for AGGRESSOR to run in the Arc, but the horse bruised a foot and was retired to stud. The first five-year-old to win the King George, AGGRESSOR amassed a total of £36,203 during his racing career. Although by no means an outstanding sire, AGGRESSOR passed on his gameness to his progeny, the best of whom was the 1974 Cheshire and Yorkshire Oaks winner Dibidale.

Petite Etoile remained in training as a five-year-old. Although she won another Coronation Cup the old sparkle was missing, and after running a disappointing race behind Le Lavanstell in the Queen Elizabeth II Stakes at Ascot she was retired to stud. To the great disappointment of her owner, Petite Etoile proved to be a dismal failure as a brood mare, producing nothing with even a glimmer of her own outstanding ability.

# 1960

## KING GEORGE VI AND QUEEN ELIZABETH STAKES

£23,345     1m 4f

July 16, 1960

| 1 | AGGRESSOR | 5 9–7 | J. Lindley. b.h. by Combat–Phaetonia |
|---|---|---|---|
| 2 | PETITE ETOILE | 4 9–4 | L. Piggott. gr.f. by Petition–Star of Iran |
| 3 | KYTHNOS | 3 8–7 | G. Lewis. b.c. by Nearula–Capital Issue |
| 4 | HIS STORY | 3 8–7 | P. Powell. ch.c. by His Slipper–Pretty Legend |
| 5 | FLORES III (FR) | 3 8–7 | R. Poincelet. ch.c. by Djebel–Caramida |
| 6 | SUNNY COURT | 4 9–7 | A. Breasley. ch.c. by Supreme Court–Sunny Eve |
| 7 | PARTHIA | 4 9–7 | W. H. Carr. b.c. by Persian Gulf–Lightning |
| 8 | DE VOOS (ITY) | 4 9–7 | J. Mercer. b.c. by Toulouse Lautrec–Dorotea Aromatari |

8 Ran

Going – Good

Distances: ½l,4l,3l,2l,½l

Time: 2:35.21

S.P. 2–5 PETITE ETOILE, 7–1 PARTHIA, 100–8 AGGRESSOR, KYTHNOS, 25–1 SUNNY COURT, 50–1 OTHERS

Winner trained by J. M. Gosden at Lewes, Sussex: owned by Sir H. Wernher: bred by Someries Stud, Newmarket

Timeform rating of winner 130

# 1961

In the year which saw the legalisation of betting shops, the 1961 King George only attracted four runners, and with two of those starting at 20–1, the race hardly provided an absorbing betting medium. Nevertheless, the two horses who disputed favouritism, St Paddy and RIGHT ROYAL V, were both top-class individuals.

RIGHT ROYAL V, who took his name from the Masefield poem, was bred by his owner Madame Elisabeth Couturie. By Owen Tudor out of Bastia, a mare who failed to win a race, he was skilfully placed by his talented trainer Etienne Pollet to win three of his four races as a two-year-old. By far the most important of these was his victory in the Grand Criterium at Longchamp, where he won unchallenged from the François Mathet-trained Moskova. At the close of the 1960 season he was rated the top two-year-old in France.

As a three-year-old he was surprisingly beaten on his reappearance when odds on for the Prix de Fontainebleau. Leaving that form well behind, RIGHT ROYAL V went on to win his next three races. An impressive victory in the Poule d'Essai des Poulains was followed by a two and a half-length success over Match III on firm going in the Prix Lupin. In extending his superiority over Match III to three lengths in the Prix du Jockey Club, RIGHT ROYAL V put up his best display of the season and earned his place in the King George line up.

St Paddy, the Noel Murless-trained son of Aureole, had landed two Classics in 1960, the Derby and the St Leger. As a four-year-old he won all three of his races prior to the King George. After easily landing the Coombe Stakes at Sandown, St Paddy went on to take the Hardwicke Stakes at Royal Ascot. Next came the Eclipse Stakes where he accounted for Proud Chieftain by a length and a half, shattering the twenty-seven-year-old Sandown mile and-a-quarter course record in the process.

St Paddy, ridden as usual by Lester Piggott, was sent off the 4–5 favourite at Ascot, with RIGHT ROYAL V a 6–4 chance. The two 20–1 shots, the temperamental Apostle and Rockavon, winner of a sub-standard Two Thousand Guineas, looked out of their depth against the two market leaders.

As the tapes went up, Poincelet settled RIGHT ROYAL V in second place, two lengths behind the frontrunner St Paddy. Although the pace was only moderate, the two outsiders were soon in trouble, struggling to lie up with the leading pair.

Half a mile from home both RIGHT ROYAL V and St Paddy appeared to be going well. At this stage Poincelet pushed his mount up to St Paddy's quarters, but Piggott responded and kicked his mount back into a two-length lead. Approaching the straight both jockeys began to ride in earnest, with Piggott the first to go for his stick. Just before the furlong marker RIGHT ROYAL V made his second challenge to St Paddy, and this time the four-year-old had no answer. Under strong pressure from Poincelet, the French raider forged clear of St Paddy to win the race by three lengths, with the other two runners virtually tailed off.

After Ascot RIGHT ROYAL V won the Prix Henri Foy before finishing second to Molvedo in the Arc.

Retired to stud at the end of the season, RIGHT ROYAL V made a sound transition from racehorse to stallion. The best of his offspring were the 1969 Irish Sweeps Derby winner Prince Regent, the 1966 Poule d'Essai des Pouliches winner Right Away, and the 1967 Yorkshire Cup winner Salvo.

RIGHT ROYAL V died in 1973.

# 1961

## KING GEORGE VI AND QUEEN ELIZABETH STAKES

£23,090     1m 4f

July 15, 1961

| | | | |
|---|---|---|---|
| 1 RIGHT ROYAL V (FR) | 3 8–7 | R. Poincelet. br.c. by Owen Tudor–Bastia |
| 2 ST PADDY | 4 9–7 | L. Piggott. b.c. by Aureole–Edie Kelly |
| 3 ROCKAVON | 3 8–7 | N. Stirk. b.c. by Rockefella–Cosmetic |
| 4 APOSTLE | 4 9–7 | E. Hide. br.c. by Blue Peter–Bellani |

4 Ran

Going – Good to Soft

Distances: 3,4,15

Time: 2:40.34

S.P. 4–5 ST PADDY, 6–4 RIGHT ROYAL V, 20–1 APOSTLE, ROCKAVON

Winner trained by Etienne Pollet at Chantilly: owned by Mme Elisabeth Couturie: bred by owner

Timeform rating of winner 135

# 1962

In 1962 François Mathet's MATCH III became the fourth French-trained winner of the King George. Bred by his owner François Dupré, MATCH III was a brown colt by the dual Arc winner Tantième, out of the Relic mare Relance III. He was thus a full brother to the Prix du Jockey Club winner Reliance II and a three parts brother to the Epsom Derby winner Relko.

A strong deep-bodied individual, MATCH III did not race as a two-year-old, but his first season on the track saw the colt win three of his seven races, the most important of which was his length and a half victory over Balbo in the French St Leger. MATCH III also ran with credit in the Prix Lupin and the Prix du Jockey Club, finishing second to the 1961 King George winner Right Royal V on both occasions.

Kept in training as a four-year-old, MATCH III started the 1962 season well with an easy victory over Star in the Prix Boiard at Saint-Cloud. Mathet's colt then put up disappointing displays in the Prix Ganay and in the Prix d'Harcourt. In the latter race MATCH III ran at least a stone below his true form, trailing in last of the ten runners. In the belief that the colt's loss of form was due to his having swallowed his tongue on these two occasions, Mathet ran him in a tongue strap in his next race, the Grand Prix de Saint-Cloud. The aid worked the oracle, MATCH III returning to form with a length and a half success over Exbury. The colt's next outing would take him across the Channel to Ascot for the King George.

MATCH III faced ten rivals at Ascot, the most dangerous of which appeared to be his compatriot, Val de Loir. As a two-year-old, Val de Loir was a stone below top class, but he improved sufficiently to land the 1962 Prix du Jockey Club in the fastest time since the war.

Unfortunately for his connections, the yielding going at Ascot would not be in Val de Loir's favour.

The best of the Irish challengers was the John Oxx-trained Arctic Storm. Successful in the 1962 Irish Two Thousand Guineas, Arctic Storm had been extremely unlucky not to make it a Classic double in the Irish Sweeps Derby, going under by a short head to Tambourine II after being hampered several times.

Noel Murless's Aurelius spearheaded the home attack. Winner of the 1961 St Leger, he was a temperamental individual prone to displays of obstinacy.

From the break, Saint-Martin took MATCH III straight into the lead, while behind him the rest of the field were closely grouped, all seemingly still going well at the halfway point. On the final bend MATCH III still held the lead with Aurelius his closest pursuer four lengths away. Once into the short Ascot straight, Breasley began to get to work on Aurelius and he pushed his mount up to MATCH III's quarters. But Saint-Martin had kept enough in reserve to repel the English challenger and at the post the French horse had three-quarters of a length to spare over Aurelius. Saint-Martin had ridden a marvellous race from the front, guiding MATCH III to become the first horse to make all in a King George.

Mathet ran MATCH III in the 1962 Arc where he finished a creditable fifth behind the three-year-old Soltikoff. He finished his racing career with a splendid victory over the American horse Kelso in the Washington International.

A truly versatile performer, MATCH III won races in three countries. He was happy to dictate the pace as he did at Ascot, or come with a late burst of speed as in the Grand Prix de Saint-Cloud. He won over £130,000 for his connections, at the time a record for a horse trained in Europe.

He died in 1965 before his capabilities as a stallion could be fully gauged.

# 1962

## KING GEORGE VI AND QUEEN ELIZABETH STAKES

£23,515      1m 4f

July 21, 1962

| | | | |
|---|---|---|---|
| 1 MATCH III (FR) | 4 | 9–7 | Y. Saint-Martin. br.c. by Tantième–Relance III |
| 2 AURELIUS | 4 | 9–7 | A. Breasley. b.c. by Aureole–Niobe II |
| 3 ARCTIC STORM | 3 | 8–7 | R. Hutchinson. br.c. by Arctic Star–Rabina |
| 4 SOVRANGO | 4 | 9–7 | W. Williamson. br.c. by Krakatao–Painted Vale |
| 5 VAL DE LOIR (FR) | 3 | 8–7 | F. Palmer. b.c. by Vieux Manoir–Vali |
| 6 VIMADEE | 4 | 9–7 | T. P. Burns. b.c. by Vimy–Upadee |
| 7 SEBRING | 3 | 8–7 | T. P. Glennon. b.c. by Aureole–Queen of Speed |
| 8 MISTI IV (FR) | 4 | 9–7 | M. Laurraun. br.c. by Medium–Mist |
| 9 WEST SIDE STORY | 3 | 8–4 | E. Smith. ch.f. by Rockefella–Red Shoes |
| 10 TRADE WIND | 3 | 8–7 | E. Hide. ch.c. by Never Say Die–Following Breeze |
| 11 RIVER CHANTER | 3 | 8–7 | J. Lindley. b.c. by Chanteur II–River Test |

11 Ran

Going – Yielding

Distances: ¾,nk,3,dh,8

Time: 2:37.02

S.P. 9–2 MATCH III, VAL DE LOIR, 11–2 AURELIUS, MISTI IV, 13–2 WEST SIDE STORY, 8–1 ARCTIC STORM, SOVRANGO, 100–8 SEBRING, 25–1 RIVER CHANTER, 50–1 VIMADEE, 100–1 TRADE WIND

Winner trained by François Mathet at Chantilly: owned by M. François Dupré: bred by owner

Timeform rating of winner 135

# 1963

As a yearling the 1963 King George winner RAGUSA looked anything but a potential champion. Bred by Captain Guggenheim at the Middleton Park Stud in County Westmeath, the son of Ribot was a small unimpressive individual. Indeed, he made such an unfavourable impression on the Captain's trainer Cecil Boyd-Rochfort, that he advised him to send the yearling to the sales. For the second time in three years the royal trainer rejected a future King George winner. It was a mistake which Boyd-Rochfort was unlikely to forget, but which Guggenheim must have taken in good spirits as part of the ups and downs of racing. The beneficiaries of the affair were trainer Paddy Prendergast and owner Jim Mullion, the pair securing the colt for the bargain-basement price of 3,800 guineas at the Ballsbridge Sales. The price reflected RAGUSA's unfurnished appearance and the fact that Ribot was still unproven as a sire.

Prendergast, a master of the art of bringing on the slow maturing thoroughbred, gave RAGUSA just one outing as a two-year-old, the colt producing a fine turn of foot to win the seven-furlong Suir Maiden Plate at the Curragh.

RAGUSA wintered well, developing into an imposing three-year-old, unrecognisable from the weedy yearling passed over by Boyd-Rochfort. He was, however, still lacking in racecourse experience, and so it caused little surprise to his connections when he finished out of the money on his seasonal reappearance, in the Players Navy Cut Trial Stakes at Phoenix Park.

Slowly but surely RAGUSA was learning how to be a racehorse. After running second to My Myosotis in the Dee Stakes at Chester, he proved himself a colt of classic standard when finishing like a train to take third place behind Relko and Merchant Venturer in the Epsom Derby.

Relko and RAGUSA were due to clash again in the Irish Sweeps Derby. Fate, however, decided otherwise. The Epsom hero was found to be lame at the start and was withdrawn, leaving RAGUSA to win comfortably by two and a half lengths from the quaintly named Vic Mo Chroi, despite the loss of a shoe six furlongs out.

Prendergast now held an extremely strong hand in the three-year-old department. In addition to RAGUSA, he also trained Noblesse, unanimously acclaimed the leading three-year-old filly in Europe after her sensational ten-length Oaks victory.

The programme mapped out for Noblesse and RAGUSA sent the filly to tackle the older horses in the King George and the colt to take in the Gordon Stakes at Goodwood. Once again Fate intervened. A week before the King George Noblesse injured her hock in an exercise spin – not a particularly serious injury but sufficient to preclude her from the Ascot race. Prendergast revised his plan. RAGUSA would now represent the stable at Ascot.

Rather surprisingly, RAGUSA did not start favourite for the big race, but was passed over in favour of the Ascot Gold Cup winner Twilight Alley. Trained by Noel Murless at Newmarket and ridden by Lester Piggott, the four-year-old was sent off the 7–2 favourite on the strength of the duo's popularity with the punters.

On form there were several other runners in with a chance of lifting the prize. Miralgo, the mount of Australian Bill Williamson, had run well in the highest class throughout the season, winning the Hardwicke Stakes and the Westbury Stakes before finishing second behind RAGUSA's stablemate Khalkis in the Eclipse.

Of the remainder, the best form belonged to Only For Life who had been the surprise winner of the 1963 Two Thousand Guineas, Soltikoff who had run a tremendous race to win the 1962 Prix de l'Arc de Triomphe, and Darling Boy who had won all three of his races prior to the King George, including a victory over Hethersett in the Jockey Club Stakes at Newmarket. However, it must be said that the absence of Relko and Noblesse, who were both injured, and of Exbury, the Coronation Cup winner, who missed the race in favour of the Grand Prix de Saint-Cloud, somewhat diminished the quality of the field.

From the off Williamson sent Miralgo into a clear lead, closely followed by Twilight Alley, RAGUSA and Only For Life. The order remained the same until four furlongs from home where RAGUSA, under his regular pilot Garnie Bougoure, moved up on the inside of Twilight Alley. At this crucial point in the race Piggott felt his horse falter and lose his action. The Gold Cup winner had split a pastern. As Piggott eased his distressed mount to a walk, the advancing Tarqogan, Darling Boy and Only For Life were severely impeded.

RAGUSA, meanwhile, with a free run, was making the best of his way home. Although Miralgo and Tarqogan ran on well in the final furlong, RAGUSA was always holding them, passing the post with four lengths to spare. The son of Ribot had become the second Irish-trained winner of the King George.

RAGUSA had two more outings after the King George, winning the Great Voltigeur Stakes at York before taking the St Leger by an effortless six lengths.

Kept in training as a four-year-old, RAGUSA added the Ardenode Stakes at Naas, and the Eclipse Stakes at Sandown to his tally of victories before ending his career in the 1964 Prix de l'Arc de Triomphe, where he finished down the field behind Prince Royal II.

During his three-season career, RAGUSA won seven races worth £146,650. He ended the 1963 season as the leading money-winner in Britain, collecting £66,011 from his three victories.

Retired to stud in Ireland, RAGUSA produced a string of top-class progeny, the best of which were probably Ragstone, winner of the Ascot Gold Cup in 1974, Caliban, successful in the 1970 Coronation Cup, and Morston the 1973 Epsom Derby winner. RAGUSA died in 1973.

Twilight Alley, the ill-fated King George favourite, went on to sire the 1978 Cheltenham Gold Cup winner Midnight Court.

# 1963

## KING GEORGE VI AND QUEEN ELIZABETH STAKES
### £28,742    1m 4f

July 20, 1963

| 1 RAGUSA | 3 8–7 | G. Bougoure. b.c. by Ribot–Fantan II |
|---|---|---|
| 2 MIRALGO (FR) | 4 9–7 | W. Williamson. ch.c. by Aureole–Nella |
| 3 TARQOGAN | 3 8–7 | A. Breasley. br.c. by Black Tarquin–Rosyogan |
| 4 DARLING BOY | 5 9–7 | J. Mercer. ch.h. by Darius–Sugar Bun |
| 5 FIGHTING SHIP | 3 8–7 | S. Smith. ch.c. by Doutelle–Jane |
| 6 NYCROS (FR) | 3 8–7 | Y. Saint-Martin. gr.c. by La Varende–First One |
| 7 SOLTIKOFF (FR) | 4 9–7 | J. Deforge. b.c. by Prince Chevalier–Aglae Grace |
| 8 ONLY FOR LIFE | 3 8–7 | J. Lindley. b.c. by Chanteur II–Life Sentence |
| 9 SOVRANGO | 5 9–7 | R. Hutchinson. br.h. by Krakatoa–Painted Vale |
| 10 TWILIGHT ALLEY | 4 9–7 | L. Piggott. ch.c. by Alycidon–Crepuscule |

10 Ran

Going – Good

Distances: 4l,5l,¾l,2l,3l

Time: 2:33.80

S.P. 7–2 TWILIGHT ALLEY, 4–1 RAGUSA, 9–2 NYCROS, 5–1 MIRALGO, 8–1 ONLY FOR LIFE, 9–1 DARLING BOY, 20–1 SOLTIKOFF, 22–1 SOVRANGO, 25–1 TARQOGAN, 50–1 FIGHTING SHIP

Winner trained by P. J. Prendergast in Ireland: owned by Mr J. R. Mullion: bred by Capt. H. F. Guggenheim in Ireland

Timeform rating of winner 137

# 1964

Only four runners went to the post in 1964. Most observers felt that the dual Derby winner Santa Claus had the race at his mercy. However, as so often happens in racing, reality was to make a mockery of the expected.

Trained in Ireland by Mick Rogers, Santa Claus started the shortest priced favourite (2–13) in the history of the King George. Having won the prestigious National Stakes as a two-year-old, he went on to score a hat trick of Classic successes in 1964 with victories in the Irish Two Thousand Guineas, the Epsom Derby (beating Indiana by a length), and in the Irish Sweeps Derby, coming home four lengths clear of Lionhearted.

Only three trainers were brave enough to take on the Irish champion. From France came the four-year-old NASRAM II, and the five-year-old Prima Donna II, while the sole English representative was the Noel Murless-trained Royal Avenue.

NASRAM II, a half-brother to Tambourine II, (winner of the inaugural Irish Sweeps Derby), was bred by his owner Mrs Howell Jackson at her Bull Run Stud in Virginia. Having failed to win a race with the son of Nasrullah as a two-year-old in America, Mrs Jackson sent him to be trained in France, initially with Etienne Pollet, and then with Ernie Fellows at Chantilly.

Prior to the King George, NASRAM II had run a series of creditable, if ultimately disappointing, races in France during the 1964 season. Placed in the Prix de Paques, the Prix Ganay, the Prix Dollar and the Grand Prix de Saint-Cloud, the bay appeared to be somewhat less than enthusiastic at the business end of his races. A natural front-runner, he continually frustrated his connections by refusing to battle once challenged. With the firm going and the short Ascot

*Above:* TULYAR (far side) partnered by Charlie Smirke tunes up for the 1952 King George.
*Below:* 1954. Her Majesty's AUREOLE beats the French challenger VAMOS in a tight finish.

*Above:* Roger Poincelet, minus cap, drives VIMY to victory in 1955.
*Below:* Enrico Camici partners mighty RIBOT in his final workout prior to the 1956 King George.

*Above:* AGGRESSOR and Jimmy Lindley upset the 5-2 on favourite PETITE ETOILE in 1960.
*Below:* RIGHT ROYAL V arrives in England to challenge for the 1961 King George.

*Above:* RAGUSA coasts home
1963.
*Below:* Bill Pyers urges
NASRAM II to victory in 196
*Top right:* AUNT EDITH, the
filly to win the King Georg
*Bottom right:* 1968. The inj
ROYAL PALACE bravely hol
off the challenge of FELICIO

*Above:* The five-year-old mare PARK TOP beats CROZIER by a length-and-a-half in 1969.
*Below:* MILL REEF and Geoff Lewis cruise to an effortless six-lengths victory in 1971.
*Right:* NIJINSKY and Lester Piggott, heroes in 1970.

*Above:* BRIGADIER GERARD holds off PARNELL to record his fifteenth successive victory.
*Below:* DAHLIA, to date the only dual King George winner.

straight in his favour, jockey Bill Pyers was determined that NASRAM II would not be given any opportunity to shirk the issue. He resolved to gallop the other three runners into the ground and, with luck, blunt Santa Claus's turn of foot.

The other French challenger, Prima Donna II, had twice been beaten convincingly by NASRAM II prior to the King George – in the Prix de Paques and in the Prix Ganay where the mare was ten lengths adrift of her rival, receiving three pounds. With no pull in the weights, Prima Donna II appeared to have little chance of reversing the form at Ascot.

The lone English challenger, Royal Avenue, had won two of his three races before the race. After beating the 1963 Two Thousand Guineas winner Only For Life in the John Porter Stakes, he won the Grand Prix du Printemps at Longchamp. Sent to Epsom for the Coronation Cup, Royal Avenue was beaten by four lengths and a head by Relko and Khalkis.

Going down to the start, Santa Claus looked ill at ease on the firm ground, while NASRAM II on the other hand, moved sweetly to the post giving his supporters cause for optimism. From the break, Pyers kicked NASRAM II into a clear lead as planned. With six furlongs to run NASRAM II led by eight lengths from his compatriot Prima Donna II, with Royal Avenue and Santa Claus a further length behind. Turning into the straight, Burke and Piggott began to make their moves as Prima Donna II rapidly lost ground. The favourite soon had the beating of Royal Avenue, but could make no impression on the leader who held on under pressure from Pyers to cross the line two lengths clear of Santa Claus.

Burke rode a poor race on the Irish champion, allowing NASRAM II too much of a lead into the straight on ground which suited front-running tactics. Had Breasley been in the saddle, as he had been at Epsom, the result may have been different. Yet, Santa Claus was undoubtedly a far better horse with some give in the ground, and in addition, he may not have fully recovered from those hard races at Epsom and the Curragh.

Both NASRAM II and Santa Claus made the trip to Longchamp for the 1964 Prix de l'Arc de Triomphe, this time the three-year-old running by far the better race to finish second, beaten three-quarters of a length by Prince Royal II with NASRAM II in the rear.

Mrs Howell Jackson ended the 1964 season as Leading Owner, having also landed the Two Thousand Guineas and Champion Stakes with Baldric II.

# 1964

## KING GEORGE VI AND QUEEN ELIZABETH STAKES

£30,740      1m 4f

July 18, 1964

| | | | |
|---|---|---|---|
| 1 NASRAM II (USA) | 4 9–7 | W. Pyers. b.c. by Nasrullah–La Mirambule | |
| 2 SANTA CLAUS | 3 8–7 | W. Burke. b.c. by Chamossaire–Aunt Clara | |
| 3 ROYAL AVENUE | 6 9–7 | L. Piggott. ch.h. by Royal Palm–Wayfarer | |
| 4 PRIMA DONNA II | 5 9–4 | M. Depalmas. b.m. by Worden II–Volti | |

4 Ran

Going – Firm

Distances: 2l,4l,4l

Time: 2:33.18

S.P. 2–13 SANTA CLAUS, 8–1 ROYAL AVENUE, 100–7 NASRAM II, 33–1 PRIMA DONNA II

Winner trained by E. Fellows in France: owned by Mrs Howell E. Jackson: bred by owner at Bull Run Stud, Virginia, USA

Timeform rating of winner 125

# 1965

Had he been sent to contest the race, Sea Bird II would probably have added the 1965 King George to his impressive list of victories. Possibly the greatest horse to race this century, the Epsom Derby winner remained in his box on the other side of the Channel while twelve inferior animals battled to land the Ascot showpiece.

Of those who did make the journey, the Paddy Prendergast-trained MEADOW COURT had by far the best credentials. The colt was part-owned by the American singer Bing Crosby and had originally been named Harwell Fool. By Court Harwell out of a moderate mare, MEADOW COURT won the seven-furlong Sandwich Maiden Stakes at Ascot on his second appearance as a two-year-old.

On his seasonal debut the colt was beaten two lengths by Western Wind in the Gladness Stakes at the Curragh. At this point, MEADOW COURT was not considered to be the best of the Prendergast three-year-olds. Great things were expected of Hardicanute, an imposing son of Hard Ridden.

In order to test the strength of the English three-year-olds, Prendergast sent MEADOW COURT to contest the Dante Stakes at York. Despite not getting a clear run, MEADOW COURT ran a promising race to finish second, a half length behind Ballymarais.

After the Dante, Hardicanute became the medium of a major gamble for the Derby. Yet within days the horse was declared a non-runner after developing a cough. Prendergast's disappointment was, however, somewhat alleviated as MEADOW COURT proved himself worthy of a place in the Epsom line-up with some impressive work on the Newbridge gallops. With Lester Piggott in the saddle for the first time, MEADOW COURT, although no match for the magnificent

Sea Bird II who was eased in the closing stages, ran on well to take second place two lengths behind the winner.

After Epsom, Prendergast always gave MEADOW COURT the benefit of a pacemaker. In his next race, the Irish Sweeps Derby, the colt scored an impressive two-length victory over Convamore. With no French challenge, MEADOW COURT was made the 6–5 favourite for the King George and of his eleven opponents, only Coronation Cup winner Oncidium, Two Thousand Guineas winner Niskar, and the 1964 Oaks winner Homeward Bound had any realistic chance of troubling the favourite.

The blinkered Khalife did a splendid job as pacemaker for MEADOW COURT, leading until two and a half furlongs out. At this stage the Geoff Lewis-ridden Soderini hit the front, closely followed by Niskar, I Say, MEADOW COURT and Homeward Bound. At the two furlong marker Piggott drove the favourite through a gap on the rails, hitting the front three hundred yards out. Despite a determined challenge from Soderini, MEADOW COURT passed the post with a two-length advantage, without coming under any real pressure from his jockey. Thus Piggott at last notched up his first King George win after so many previous disappointments in the race. MEADOW COURT provided Paddy Prendergast with his second success having taken the honours with Ragusa in 1963.

MEADOW COURT went to Doncaster the 4–11 favourite for the St Leger. Unable to handle the bottomless going, he was soundly beaten by ten lengths by the Dick Hern-trained Provoke. Not surprisingly, he was comprehensively outpointed by Sea Bird II in the Arc, coming home a respectable ninth of twenty.

At the end of the 1965 season, MEADOW COURT was rated fourteen pounds below Sea Bird II in the Free Handicap. Prendergast's horse can thus be judged a most fortunate King George winner.

Retired to Sandley Stud in Dorset, MEADOW COURT had little success as a sire and was exported to Canada in 1969.

# 1965

## KING GEORGE VI AND QUEEN ELIZABETH STAKES
### £31,207    1m 4f

July 17, 1965

| | | | | |
|---|---|---|---|---|
| 1 | MEADOW COURT | 3 8–7 | L. Piggott. ch.c. by Court Harwell–Meadow Music | |
| 2 | SODERINI | 4 9–7 | G. Lewis. b.c. by Crepello–Matuta | |
| 3 | ONCIDIUM | 4 9–7 | W. Williamson b.c. by Alcide–Malcolmia | |
| 4 | NISKAR | 3 8–7 | D. Smith. ch.c. by Le Haar–Niskampe | |
| 5 | I CLAUDIUS | 6 9–7 | F. Durr. b.h. by Tantième–Armada | |
| 6 | HOMEWARD BOUND | 4 9–4 | G. Starkey. ch.f. by Alycidon–Sabie River | |
| 7 | KHALIFE (BL) | 3 8–7 | J. Roe. ch.c. by Montaval–Jill Scott | |
| 8 | INDIANA | 4 9–7 | J. Lindley. b.c. by Sayajirao–Willow Ann | |
| 9 | I SAY | 3 8–7 | R. Poincelet. br.c. by Sayajirao–Isetta | |
| 10 | WESTERN WIND | 3 8–7 | L. Ward. ch.c. by Milesian–Palestrina | |
| 11 | BALLY JOY | 4 9–7 | J. Purtell. b.c. by Ballymoss–Gladness | |
| 12 | BISCAYNE (BL) | 4 9–7 | R. Hutchinson. b.c. by Talgo–Marjorie Castle | |

12 Ran

Going – Good

Distances: 21,31,51,61,2½l

Time: 2:33.27

S.P. 6–5 MEADOW COURT, 5–1 ONCIDIUM, 13–2 I SAY, 100–9 SODERINI, 100–7 INDIANA, HOMEWARD BOUND, 25–1 NISKAR, BALLY JOY, WESTERN WIND, 66–1 BISCAYNE, 100–1 OTHERS

Winner trained by P. J. Prendergast in Ireland: owned by Mr M. Bell: bred by Mrs E. Parker Poe

Timeform rating of winner 129

# 1966

The 1966 season brought the break-up of one of the most successful jockey-trainer partnerships in the history of the Turf. Lester Piggott's determination to ride Vincent O'Brien's Valoris in the Oaks in preference to the Noel Murless-trained Varina, resulted in the dissolution of a ten-year association which had yielded six English Classic victories and a host of other Group race successes. In truth, the "split" was not as definitive as it at first appeared. Although the old intimacy had been broken, Lester continued to ride for Murless "when available". Piggott made sure he was free to partner the Murless-trained AUNT EDITH in the King George.

AUNT EDITH, a chestnut filly by Primera, took time to develop, brought along slowly by her trainer. Unplaced in both of her races as a two-year-old, she improved steadily during her second season. After running a promising second in the Musidora, AUNT EDITH went on to win the Nassau Stakes at Goodwood and the Prix Vermeille at Longchamp.

With her regular partner, Piggott, in the saddle, the Murless filly started her four-year-old season with an impressive victory in the Yorkshire Cup, beating the future Ascot Gold Cup winner Fighting Charlie by a comfortable four lengths after making all the running. In her next race, the Hardwicke Stakes, AUNT EDITH suffered a surprising defeat at the hands of the Paddy Prendergast-trained Prominer. Never going well, the filly finished a poor fifth of six, over fourteen lengths behind the winner. A routine dope test proved negative. The Murless team were baffled but decided to let AUNT EDITH take her chance in the King George where she would meet Prominer on ten pounds better terms.

An outbreak of swamp fever resulted in restrictions on horses entering Britain from abroad, and so there were no French challengers for the 1966 Ascot showpiece. Yet although AUNT EDITH faced only four opponents, her task was by no means a simple one.

Apart from Prominer, who was fancied by his connections to maintain the Hardwicke form, Piggott's mount had to contend with formidable challenges from the Irish Sweeps Derby winner Sodium and the ex-American Hill Rise. Hill Rise, a stable companion of AUNT EDITH, won twelve of his thirty-four races in the USA, including a victory in the prestigious Man O'War Stakes. He had also run a neck second to Northern Dancer in the 1964 Kentucky Derby. He had settled down well at Warren Place, notching up a Royal Ascot success in the Rous Memorial Stakes, where he beat the useful Silly Season by a head. The King George would test his mettle to the full. The fifth member of the field, Vrai, although a useful horse in his own right, was to make the pace for his stable companion Prominer.

From the break, Wally Swinburn kicked Vrai into a twelve-length lead and soon had the field strung out in Indian file. Piggott made his move on AUNT EDITH at Swinley Bottom, taking the lead two and a half out. At this point Vrai had given his all and faded dramatically. At the two furlong marker AUNT EDITH was challenged by both Prominer and Sodium. The Irish horse was the first to crack, leaving Piggott and Durr on Sodium to fight out the finish. Inside the final furlong, Sodium put in a spirited challenge, but the filly responded gamely to Piggott's calls and crossed the line a half-length ahead of her rival. Prominer, unable to reproduce his Hardwicke form finished third, two lengths behind Sodium. Hill Rise ran a most disappointing race beating only the pacemaker Vrai. AUNT EDITH had become the first filly to win a King George.

Sodium went on to frank the King George form by winning the St Leger by a head from the Derby winner Charlottown.

AUNT EDITH took her place in the 1966 Arc, but despite starting favourite, she could finish no better than eighth behind the French-trained Bon Mott III. In November she was sold to Ogden Phipps, Chairman of the New York Jockey Club, for $185,000.

# 1966

## KING GEORGE VI AND QUEEN ELIZABETH STAKES

£29,167     1m 4f

July 16, 1966

| 1 AUNT EDITH | 4 9–4 | L. Piggott. ch.f. by Primera–Fair Edith |
|---|---|---|
| 2 SODIUM | 3 8–7 | F. Durr. b.c. by Psidium–Gambade |
| 3 PROMINER | 4 9–7 | D. Lake. ch.c. by Beau Sabreur–Snob Hill |
| 4 HILL RISE | 5 9–7 | W. Rickaby. b.h. by Hilary–Red Curtain |
| 5 VRAI | 3 8–7 | W. Swinburn. b.c. by Die Hard–Verity |

5 Ran

Going – Good

Distances: ½l,2l,1½l,20l

Time: 2:35.06

S.P. 6–4 SODIUM, 7–2 AUNT EDITH, 4–1 PROMINER, HILL RISE, 33–1 VRAI

Winner trained by N. Murless at Newmarket: owned by Mr J. Hornung: bred by West Grinstead Stud

Timeform rating of winner 126

# 1967

BUSTED was one of those horses who needed time. Bred by his owner Mr Stanhope Joel at his Snailwell Stud in Newmarket, the big bay son of Crepello did not reach his peak as a racehorse until his fourth year.

Originally trained in Ireland by Brud Featherstonhaugh, BUSTED's two racecourse appearances as a juvenile gave little indication of the tremendous ability he would later display. After finishing a well-beaten sixth of fourteen on his debut at the Curragh, BUSTED ran ninth of twelve in the Larkspur Stakes at Leopardstown.

Stanhope Joel's horse started his second season well, winning the Gallinule Stakes over ten furlongs at the Curragh. Unfortunately, that proved to be his only success of the season. After running second in the Desmond Stakes, BUSTED finished down the field in both the Irish Sweeps Derby and the Irish Cambridgeshire. At the close of the 1966 season Stanhope Joel decided to transfer the horse to Noel Murless at Newmarket. It proved to be an inspired decision.

Under Murless's guidance, BUSTED went through the 1967 season unbeaten. After winning the Coronation Stakes at Sandown by an effortless three lengths, the handsome bay went on to destroy a talented field in the Eclipse, coming home two and a half lengths clear of Great Nephew without coming off the bit. The King George would prove just how much improvement BUSTED had made during his fourth year.

Stable jockey George Moore was reunited with BUSTED at Ascot. The Australian had opted to ride the stable's One Thousand Guineas winner Fleet in the Eclipse, leaving the veteran Bill Rickaby to partner the colt. Rickaby had played a major role in BUSTED's development, patiently teaching the big horse his craft during spins on the Newmarket gallops.

The 1967 King George field was one of the strongest ever assembled, with no less than four Derby winners and the 1966 Prix de l'Arc de Triomphe winner going to the post.

Somewhat surprisingly, the enigmatic Ribocco started favourite at Ascot. After topping the Free Handicap as a juvenile, the son of Ribot had proved disappointing in the Craven Stakes at Newmarket and the Dee Stakes at Chester. Tried in blinkers in the Lingfield Derby Trial, he again failed to shine, finishing fifth to the moderate Heave Ho. Most observers concluded that he had failed to train on. However, in the three weeks between Lingfield and Epsom, Ribocco began to show his old sparkle at home. With Piggott in the saddle, the colt ran a fine race in the Derby, coming off the pace to finish second, beaten by two and a half lengths by Jim Joel's Royal Palace. The improvement continued. Fulke Johnson-Houghton sent Ribocco to the Curragh for the Irish Sweeps Derby where he comfortably beat the Murless-trained Sucaryl by three-quarters of a length. Ribocco was to meet his elders for the first time at Ascot.

The other Irish Sweeps Derby winner in the field was the George Todd-trained Sodium. Keeping a Classic winner in training as a four-year-old is always a somewhat risky business and in the case of Sodium, the risk did not pay dividends. The son of Psidium lined up at Ascot with little chance of success after having been beaten comprehensively by Salvo in the Hardwicke Stakes, and by BUSTED in the Eclipse.

In contrast, the 1966 Prix du Jockey Club winner Nelcius appeared to hold sound claims on his second to Charlottown in the Coronation Cup. The French raider had both Jolly Jet and Sodium in arrears at Epsom and at identical weights held every prospect of finishing in front of the pair at Ascot. Nelcius started a popular third favourite behind Ribocco and BUSTED.

The other French representative. Bon Mott III, had beaten twenty-three rivals to land the 1966 Prix de l'Arc de Triomphe. The chestnut's best effort in 1967 prior to the King George was a workmanlike victory in the Prix de Lutece at Longchamp in May, beating the filly Parthian Glance by two and a half lengths. The Worden II colt needed to return to his three-year-old form to trouble the market leaders at Ascot.

The fourth Derby winner in the field was the four-year-old Appiani II, trained, like Ribot, by Ugo Penco. Winner of the Italian

Derby in 1966, the son of Herbager had been unlucky in running when beaten by a head in the Gran Premio di Milano. In his only race in Britain prior to the King George, Appiani II ran a creditable third behind BUSTED and Great Nephew, beaten only by four lengths in the Eclipse Stakes.

The Harry Wragg-trained Salvo was an interesting candidate. After going down by a head to the 1966 Derby winner Charlottown in the John Porter Stakes, the four-year-old put up two highly impressive performances – in the Yorkshire Cup where he beat Mintmaster by five lengths and in the Hardwicke Stakes at Royal Ascot, beating Sodium by a clever half-length under an inspired ride from Ron Hutchinson. The second Wragg representative in the King George, the handicapper Calisto, was to act as pacemaker.

In the early stages of the race, Calisto and Jolly Jet shared the lead, setting a strong gallop. The serious contenders were content to sit in behind the two leaders until the race began in earnest. As the field swung into Swinley Bottom, Nelcius suddenly lost his place in behind the two leaders. Gilbert, fearing his mount had broken a blood vessel, eased Nelcius to a walk, hampering Ribocco in the process. At this point Calisto and Jolly Jet had given their all and weakened quickly. Seeing his chance to get first run on his rivals, Hutchinson kicked Salvo into a four-length lead. With two furlongs to run, Appiani II, Bon Mott III, and BUSTED, formed a three-pronged challenge to the leader. The surge of the two overseas challengers was short-lived, leaving Salvo and BUSTED to fight out the finish. At the distance, BUSTED gained the upper hand and went on to pass the post three lengths clear of Salvo, with the fast-finishing Ribocco in third.

A post-race examination found Nelcius to be perfectly sound. Incredibly, the horse's trainer, Clement, claimed his charge had suffered sunstroke during the race, an excuse which must go down in the record books as the most implausible ever offered for a horse's defeat.

BUSTED provided Murless with his second consecutive King George after Aunt Edith's win the previous year. With Royal Palace landing the Two Thousand Guineas and the Derby, and Fleet the One Thousand Guineas, the Warren Place trainer ended the 1967 season as Champion Trainer, bringing the title back to England after four years of Irish domination.

After Ascot, BUSTED went on to land the Prix Henri Foy at Longchamp before being retired to his owner's stud at a fee of 2,000 guineas. As the sire of such outstanding performers as the 1974 St Leger winner Bustino, and the 1988 King George hero Mtoto, BUSTED was rightly considered to be a stallion of the highest class. He died of a heart attack in March 1988.

## 1967

## KING GEORGE VI AND QUEEN ELIZABETH STAKES

£24,369     1m 4f

July 15, 1967

| 1 BUSTED | 4 9–7 | G. Moore, b.c. by Crepello–Sans Le Sou |
|---|---|---|
| 2 SALVO | 4 9–7 | R. Hutchinson. ch.c. by Right Royal V–Soirée |
| 3 RIBOCCO | 3 8–7 | L. Piggott. b.c. by Ribot–Easy Eight |
| 4 APPIANI II (ITY) | 4 9–7 | C. Ferrari. b.c. by Herbager–Angela Rucellai |
| 5 BON MOTT III (FR) | 4 9–7 | A. Head. ch.c. by Worden II–Djebel Idra |
| 6 SODIUM | 4 9–7 | A. Breasley. b.c. by Psidium–Gambade |
| 7 JOLLY JET (USA) (BL) | 4 9–7 | W. Williamson. ch.c. by Jet Action–La Joliette |
| 8 CALISTO | 4 9–7 | W. Snaith. b.c. by Petition–Cold Response |
| 9 NELCIUS (FR) | 4 9–7 | A. Gilbert. br.c. by Tenareze–Namagua |

9 Ran

Going – Good

Distances: 3l,nk,sht hd,4l,2l

Time: 2:33.64

S.P. 5–2 RIBOCCO, 4–1 BUSTED, 7–1 NELCIUS, 15–2 SODIUM, 8–1 BON MOTT III, SALVO, APPIANI II, 33–1 JOLLY JET, 200–1 CALISTO

Winner trained by N. Murless at Newmarket: owned by Mr S. Joel: bred by the Snailwell Stud Co.

Timeform rating of winner 134

# 1968

For the third successive year the King George went to an inmate of Noel Murless's Warren Place yard, an unprecedented hat trick of victories. In common with Murless's previous King George winners, Aunt Edith and Busted, ROYAL PALACE landed the Ascot prize in his fourth year.

An attractive bay colt by the 1958 King George winner Ballymoss, ROYAL PALACE was far and away the best-staying two-year-old in Britain in 1966, with victories in the Acomb Stakes and the Royal Lodge Stakes to his credit.

ROYAL PALACE should have landed the Triple Crown in 1967. After beating Taj Dewan in the Two Thousand Guineas, Jim Joel's colt turned in a marvellous performance in the Derby. Under an inspirational ride from Australian George Moore, ROYAL PALACE left a high-class field for dead, coming home with two and a half lengths to spare over the Lester Piggott-ridden Ribocco. The Murless horse seemed to have the St Leger, and therefore the Triple Crown, at his mercy; but sadly it was not to be. Only three weeks before Doncaster ROYAL PALACE suffered an injury which kept him out of the race and in his final appearance as a three-year-old the colt finished third behind Reform and Taj Dewan in the Champion Stakes.

ROYAL PALACE returned to his customary winning ways with a smooth victory over Sidon in the 1968 Coronation Stakes at Sandown. After beating his solitary opponent in the Prince of Wales Stakes, ROYAL PALACE gave his supporters a fright when coming with a devastating late run to snatch the Eclipse Stakes in the last strides from his old rival Taj Dewan and the Derby winner Sir Ivor.

Neither of ROYAL PALACE's Sandown victims renewed rivalry in the King George. Of his six opponents at Ascot, two were trained in England, two in France and two in Italy.

The English challenge was spearheaded by Lester Piggott's mount Ribero. By the great Ribot out of Libra, Ribero was thus a full brother to Ribocco, the disappointing 1967 King George favourite. On his previous run, Ribero had upset the odds laid on Sir Ivor in the Irish Sweeps Derby, coming home two lengths clear of the O'Brien horse. The other English-trained runner, Tapis Rose, was a 50–1 chance and appeared hopelessly outclassed.

From France came the three-year-old Felicio II, and the year older Topyo. The Maurice Zilber-trained Felicio II was very much the Gallic second string despite filling the runner-up position in both the Prix de Fontainebleau and the Prix Lupin. Topyo, the main French hope, had won the 1967 Arc but had failed to catch the judge's eye in his last three races prior to the King George.

From Italy came Carlos Primero, winner of the 1967 Italian St Leger, accompanied by his stable companion and intended pace-maker, Golden Fizz II.

The temperamental Ribero dislodged Piggott on the way to the post, causing the start to be delayed by ten minutes, but once the race was off, Golden Fizz II, as anticipated, broke smartly and soon held a commanding advantage. In behind, Barclay and Piggott played a game of cat and mouse, each wary of the other. As the field reached Swinley Bottom, Piggott kicked for home on Ribero, moving smoothly past the two Italian raiders. The mouse had made his move; the cat was ready to pounce.

In the home straight, Ribero's stride started to shorten as ROYAL PALACE made rapid progress. With a furlong to run ROYAL PALACE took the lead and appeared to have the race by the scruff of the neck. Then suddenly there was a tremendous gasp from the packed grandstand as ROYAL PALACE began to falter and hang away from the rails. The favourite had torn suspensory ligaments in his near fore. Barclay was on the horns of a dilemma. The winning post was agonisingly close. Should he use his stick to urge on his mount or should he sit and suffer and nurse him home? To his eternal credit the youthful Barclay chose the latter course of action, holding his injured mount together and keeping him well balanced.

Sensing the favourite was in trouble, the two French jockeys frantically gave chase. Under a torrent of strokes from Poincelet, Felicio II began to inch closer and closer to the injured ROYAL PALACE. With a masterly display of horsemanship Barclay coaxed

[ 72 ]

ROYAL PALACE over the finishing line, a precious half-length ahead of his snapping French pursuers. Another twenty yards and the prize would have crossed the Channel.

The gallant King George hero retired to the Egerton Stud, the winner of nine of his eleven races, with earnings in excess of £166,000.

The best of his offspring were undoubtedly the 1977 Oaks and St Leger – winning filly Dunfermline and the triple Champion Hurdler See You Then. ROYAL PALACE retired from stallion duties in 1987.

# 1968

## KING GEORGE VI AND QUEEN ELIZABETH STAKES

£24,020    1m 4f

July 27, 1968

| | | | |
|---|---|---|---|
| 1 ROYAL PALACE | 4 | 9–7 | A. Barclay. b.c. by Ballymoss–Crystal Palace |
| 2 FELICIO II (FR) | 3 | 8–7 | R. Poincelet, br.c. by Shantung–Fighting Edie |
| 3 TOPYO (FR) | 4 | 9–7 | W. Pyers. b.c. by Fine Top–Delirosa |
| 4 RIBERO | 3 | 8–7 | L. Piggott. b.c. by Ribot–Libra |
| 5 TAPIS ROSE | 4 | 9–7 | A. Breasley. b.c. by Tissot–Rosace |
| 6 CARLOS PRIMERO (ITY) | 4 | 9–7 | G. Dettori. b.c. by Janitor–Charlotte |
| 7 GOLDEN FIZZ II (ITY) | 4 | 9–7 | M. Cipolloni. ch.c. by Tenerani–Galceda |

7 Ran

Going – Firm

Distances: ½,sht hd,5,12,6

Time: 2:33.22

S.P. 4–7 ROYAL PALACE, 9–4 RIBERO, 100–9 TOPYO, 20–1 CARLOS PRIMERO, 28–1 FELICIO II, 50–1 TAPIS ROSE, 100–1 GOLDEN FIZZ II

Winner trained by Noel Murless at Newmarket: owned by Mr H. J. Joel: bred by owner

Timeform rating of winner 131

# 1969

I n an age when it is fashionable to rush our top-class horses off to stud after their second season, how satisfying it is to remember PARK TOP, one of the best post-war middle-distance fillies, who reached her peak at the grand old age of five.

PARK TOP was a late foal (May 27) with rather round fetlock joints. By the unfashionable Kalydon out of the "useless" Nellie Park, she was very much one of the lesser lights at the 1965 Tattersalls' October Sales. Newmarket trainer Bernard van Cutsem, who had trained Kalydon, picked up the filly at her reserve price of 500 guineas. Andrew, 11th Duke of Devonshire, had owned the dam Nellie Park, who, despite her poor racing record, was a half-sister to the useful sprinter Pappa Fourway. Van Cutsem offered the filly to the Duke who, after initial reservations, became the owner of the future "Racehorse of the Year".

As a two-year-old, PARK TOP damaged her near hock, and suffered the cough which kept her off the racecourse. The setback was, however, a blessing in disguise, allowing her to develop physically without having to endure the rigours of premature competition.

When she finally reached the racetrack as a three-year-old in 1967, PARK TOP made up for lost time by winning her first four races. By far the most impressive of these victories came in the Ribblesdale Stakes at Royal Ascot, where she beat the One Thousand Guineas and Oaks runner-up St Pauli Girl by half a length.

Although PARK TOP won two races as a four-year-old, the Brighton Challenge Cup and the Prix d'Hedouville, she was beaten on five other occasions, seemingly without excuse. But in 1969, as a five-year-old, PARK TOP enjoyed a golden season. After landing the Prix de la Seine in May, the mare put up a breathtaking performance to win the Coronation Cup by three-quarters of a length from Mount Athos and Connaught.

Next came the Hardwicke Stakes where, ridden by Geoff Lewis in place of the suspended Lester Piggott, PARK TOP easily accounted for Chicago by one and a half lengths. Lewis retained the ride in the Eclipse. Piggott had chosen to ride Ribofilio but switched to the Henry Cecil-trained Wolver Hollow when the Ribot colt was found to be coughing.

Lewis did not ride one of his better races that day at Sandown. In a seven-horse field he managed to get PARK TOP boxed in behind weakening rivals as Piggott kicked for home on Wolver Hollow. The mare fought bravely but could not peg back Wolver Hollow, who having obtained first run, held on by two and a half lengths.

Needless to say, Piggott was back aboard PARK TOP for her next race, the King George. Although van Cutsem's stable had been hit by the virus during June and July, PARK TOP had fortunately remained unaffected and lined up at Ascot in magnificent condition.

Apart from PARK TOP, the 1969 King George field was one of the weakest ever assembled. Neither the Epsom Derby winner Blakeney nor the Oaks heroine Sleeping Partner was in the field; in fact the Classic generation failed to provide any representative at all.

Of her eight opponents, PARK TOP had already beaten Crozier, Timmy My Boy, Chicago, and the Italian entry Hogarth. The Japanese representative Speed Symboli and the French challenger Soyeux were not up to Group One standard and Coolroy was in the field as pacemaker for Chicago. Thus the mare's only serious rival appeared to be the Maurice Zilber-trained four-year-old Felicio II who had finished second to Royal Palace in the 1968 King George. Winner of the 1969 Grand Prix de Saint-Cloud, the Shantung colt shared favouritism with PARK TOP at 9–4.

As the Ascot crowd basked in glorious sunshine, PARK TOP moved beautifully down to the start. Last into the stalls, Piggott allowed his mount to miss the break slightly in order to switch her off at the rear of the field.

After nine furlongs the pacemaker Coolroy still held the lead, closely followed by Speed Symboli, Timmy My Boy, Hogarth and Crozier. At the rear of the field came the two market leaders, both jockeys looking to come with a late run.

As the field swung wide around the final turn, a gap appeared on the inside. Piggott eased PARK TOP through, the mare improving from last to first in an instant. With Piggott sitting motionless, PARK TOP toyed with her rivals before striding away to pass the post a length and a half clear of the hard-ridden Crozier. Hogarth just got the better of the disappointing Felicio II for third place.

After Ascot PARK TOP went on to land the Prix Henri Foy before finishing a desperately unlucky second to the Ascot Gold Cup winner Levmoss in the Arc. With Piggott riding one of his less distinguished races, PARK TOP came with a tremendous late run, failing by only three-quarters of a length, after being in an impossible position turning for home. In her final race of 1969 PARK TOP was surprisingly beaten by the French filly Flossy in the Champion Stakes.

At the end of the season, PARK TOP was voted "Racehorse of the Year", only the second female to be so honoured, Petite Etoile being the first.

Kept in training as a six-year-old, PARK TOP suffered from fragile fetlocks yet still managed to win Longchamp's La Coupe and the Cumberland Lodge Stakes at Ascot.

Retired to the paddocks at the end of the 1970 season, PARK TOP proved a failure as a brood mare, producing only one minor winner from just three live foals. She died in May 1989, just seventeen days short of her twenty-fifth birthday.

# 1969

## KING GEORGE VI AND QUEEN ELIZABETH STAKES

£31,122      1m 4f

July 26, 1969

| | | | |
|---|---|---|---|
| 1 PARK TOP | 5 | 9–4 | L. Piggott. b.m. by Kalydon–Nellie Park |
| 2 CROZIER | 6 | 9–7 | D. Keith. b.h. by Zarathustra–Vimere |
| 3 HOGARTH (ITY) | 4 | 9–7 | C. Ferrari. b.c. by Neckar–Hopeful Duchess |
| 4 FELICIO II (b) | 4 | 9–7 | W. Pyers. br.c. by Shantung–Fighting Edie |
| 5 SPEED SYMBOLI (JAP) | 6 | 9–7 | Y. Nohira. b.h. by Royal Challenger–Sweet In |
| 6 TIMMY MY BOY (b) | 4 | 9–7 | A. Barclay. b.c. by Tompion–Pink Silk |
| 7 SOYEUX (FR) | 4 | 9–7 | R. Poincelet. ch.c. by Fils de Roi–Sauvage |
| 8 CHICAGO | 5 | 9–7 | R. Hutchinson. b.h. by Fidalgo–Grischuna |
| 9 COOLROY | 8 | 9–7 | G. Starkey, b.h. by Saint Crespin III–Emali |

9 Ran

Going – Firm

Distances: 1½,nk,3,4,3,2½

Time: 2:32.46

S.P. 9–I PARK TOP, FELICIO II, 6–I TIMMY MY BOY, 8–I CHICAGO, 10–I SOYEUX, 20–I HOGARTH, 25–I SPEED SYMBOLI, 28–I CROZIER, 150–I COOLROY

Winner trained by B. van Cutsem at Newmarket: owned by Duke of Devonshire: bred by Mrs L. Scott

Timeform rating of winner 131

# 1970

The fact that Triple Crown winner NIJINSKY came into the ownership of platinum tycoon Charles Engelhard and under the care of trainer Vincent O'Brien, was brought about by a combination of circumstance and O'Brien's uncanny eye for a potential champion.

Engelhard sent O'Brien to the 1968 Woodbine Sales in Toronto to check out a Ribot colt he had chosen. The Tipperary trainer rejected the Ribot yearling due to a malformation of the foreleg. At this point Fate took a hand in the proceedings, allowing O'Brien to be in the right place at the right time.

Amongst the many yearlings on offer was a lovely Northern Dancer colt sent up by E. P. Taylor of Windfields Farm. The bay made such an impression on O'Brien that he determined to secure him for his patron. $84,000 clinched the deal, and what an inspired purchase it proved to be. The Ribot colt turned out to be moderate while the son of Northern Dancer went on to become the first Triple Crown winner to be purchased at public auction.

NIJINSKY won all five of his races as a two-year-old, culminating in an impressive three-length victory in the Dewhurst Stakes.

Charles Engelhard had owned top-class horses in the past, notably Ribocco, Ribero and Indiana, but in NIJINSKY he knew he had a potential world-beater. That potential was realised with interest as the handsome bay strode majestically through the summer of 1970.

NIJINSKY wintered well under O'Brien's skilful care, and arrived at Newmarket the shortest priced favourite for the Two Thousand Guineas since Colombo in 1934. The 4–7 chance never looked in the slightest danger of defeat, accounting for the useful Yellow God by an effortless two and a half lengths.

At Epsom in June NIJINSKY started at odds against for the only time in his career. Piggott coaxed another breathtaking performance from the Guineas winner who only needed to be shaken up to beat the French colt Gyr by two and a half lengths in the fastest Derby since electronic recording began. The Derby form was made to look rock solid when Gyr went on to win the Grand Prix de Saint-Cloud.

NIJINSKY's next race was the Irish Sweeps Derby at the Curragh, where his unbeaten record was easily maintained with a comprehensive defeat of Meadowville. As in the colt's previous races in Ireland he was partnered by stable jockey Liam Brown while Piggott watched from a respectful distance on the runner-up.

And so the stage was set for a memorable King George. NIJINSKY, with his unbeaten record, was the only three-year-old in the field, having scared away all of his contemporaries. He would, however, be fully tested by the best older horses in Europe. The field of six included three Derby winners – NIJINSKY, Blakeney and the 1968 Italian Derby winner Hogarth who had finished third behind Park Top in the previous year's King George. The remaining three runners had each proved themselves in the highest class, Karabas having won the 1969 Washington International, Crepellana the 1969 French Oaks and Caliban the 1970 Coronation Cup.

Piggott was reunited with NIJINSKY for the Ascot race, but only after the maestro had been involved in an injury scare. The "long fellow" had been thrown at Newbury in June, sustaining broken bones in his foot; physiotherapy and ice treatment hastened his recovery and he was able to take the ride on the favourite.

Ascot has been the scene of countless outstanding performances, but on this July day in 1970 NIJINSKY was truly majestic. He treated his elders like selling-platers, producing the most impressive display of his illustrious career.

While Hogarth was smartly away, leading for the first furlong, Lester was content to keep his mount at the rear of the field. After two furlongs Caliban took over the lead with his rivals bunched up close behind. There was little change in the order until the field swept round the final turn into the straight, where Karabas made his move on the outside of Caliban, with Hogarth between the pair. With two furlongs to run Karabas gained a slight advantage with Blakeney and Crepellana gaining ground on the inside. NIJINSKY, meanwhile, had been making relentless progress from the rear of the field. With just over a furlong to run Piggott switched to the centre of the track and in a matter of strides had the race won, taking the lead in the final furlong, still on the bridle. Lester even had time to look around for non-existent dangers. Such was NIJINSKY's superiority that he was eased close home. The winning margin of two lengths over the hard-ridden Blakeney could easily have been doubled. The disappointment of the race was second favourite Caliban who faded dramatically in the final two furlongs.

NIJINSKY had beaten his five rivals in a time two seconds outside the average, and six seconds outside Park Top's course record, Nevertheless it was a first-class performance by a horse who was clearly at the very peak of his form.

After the King George, the press labelled NIJINSKY "the Horse of the Century", and suggested that the St Leger was a foregone conclusion. Their optimism proved well placed. By beating his old rival Meadowville at Doncaster, NIJINSKY became the first Triple Crown winner since Bahram in 1935. Remarkably Charles Engelhard's champion never won another race.

On all known form NIJINSKY should have added the Prix de l'Arc de Triomphe to his long list of victories and yet, in the event, he was beaten by a head by Sassafras. Most observers blamed Piggott for this unexpected defeat, arguing that he gave NIJINSKY far too much ground to make up at the end of a fast-run race. In reality a combination of a bad draw, the debilitating effects of ringworm and the cumulative pressures of a long season had taken the edge off the horse.

If NIJINSKY had won the Arc he would have been retired as the undefeated champion of Europe. After his defeat at Longchamp, connections decided to give the horse a chance to bow out in a blaze of glory in the Champion Stakes. Again NIJINSKY ran well below his true form. After sweating up badly at the start, he eventually went down by one and a half lengths to the Noel Murless-trained Lorenzaccio.

At the close of the 1970 season NIJINSKY's career record stood at eleven wins from thirteen starts, with total earnings of £238,615.

Despite the valiant efforts of a syndicate created by the Thoroughbred Breeders' Associations of England, Ireland and France, there was never any realistic prospect of NIJINSKY taking up his stud career in Europe, such was the influence of the dollar.

Valued at five and a half million dollars, NIJINSKY retired to

Claiborne Farm in Kentucky with a full book of classically bred mares. With progeny of the calibre of Epsom Derby winners Golden Fleece and Shahrastani, Prix du Jockey Club winner Caerleon and American Stakes winner Ferdinand, NIJINSKY has established himself as a first-rate stallion on both sides of the Atlantic.

## KING GEORGE VI AND QUEEN ELIZABETH STAKES
## (GROUP ONE)

£31,993      1m 4f

July 25, 1970

| | | |
|---|---|---|
| 1 NIJINSKY (CAN) | 3 8–7 | L. Piggott. b.c. by Northern Dancer–Flaming Page |
| 2 BLAKENEY | 4 9–7 | G. Lewis. b.c. by Hethersett–Windmill Girl |
| 3 CREPELLANA (FR) | 4 9–4 | J. Duforge. ch.f. by Crepello–Astana |
| 4 KARABAS | 5 9–7 | W. Williamson, b.h. by Worden II–Fair Share |
| 5 HOGARTH (ITY) | 5 9–7 | C. Ferrari. b.h. by Neckar–Hopeful Duchess |
| 6 CALIBAN | 4 9–7 | A. Barclay. b.c. by Ragusa–Island Lore |

6 Ran

Going – Good

Distances: 2l,4l,1l,5l,1½l

Time: 2:36.16

S.P. 40–85 NIJINSKY, 5–I CALIBAN, I3–2 KARABAS, IOO–7 BLAKENEY, 20–I CREPELLANA, 33–I HOGARTH

Winner trained by M. V. O'Brien at Cashel, Co Tipperary: owned by Mr C. Engelhard: bred by Mr E. P. Taylor in Canada

Timeform rating of winner 138

# 1971

Two outstanding performers shared centre stage throughout the 1971 season, MILL REEF and Brigadier Gerard. At the time, opinion was fiercely divided as to which was the superior racehorse. With the benefit of hindsight, MILL REEF is now recognised as one of the best mile and a half performers to have graced the English turf, while Brigadier Gerard is deservedly acknowledged a champion over eight to ten furlongs.

MILL REEF was bred by his owner Paul Mellon at his Rokeby Farm Stud in Virginia. By Never Bend out of Milan Mill, Mellon named the bay colt after a geological formation off the coast of Antigua.

As a yearling, MILL REEF was considered to be too long in the pastern to be suited to the American dirt tracks and so the decision was made to send the horse to race in England, in the care of Kingsclere trainer Ian Balding.

Under the experienced tuition of Balding, MILL REEF developed into an outstanding two-year-old. After picking up a small race at Salisbury on his racecourse debut, the bay went on to record a spectacular series of victories, capturing the Coventry Stakes, the Imperial Stakes, the Gimcrack Stakes and the Dewhurst Stakes. MILL REEF's only defeat during the 1970 season came in the Prix Robert Papin at Maisons-Laffite where he went down by a short head to the previously unbeaten My Swallow. At the close of a vintage season for English-trained two-year-olds, MILL REEF was rated one pound behind My Swallow, and one pound ahead of Brigadier Gerard in the Free Handicap.

Although he never grew beyond 15.3 hands, MILL REEF looked magnificent on his seasonal reappearance in the Greenham Stakes at Newbury. Making all the running, the little horse disposed of the useful Breeder's Dream by an effortless four lengths. All thoughts now turned to the Two Thousand Guineas where MILL REEF would meet My Swallow and Brigadier Gerard in what was billed as "the clash of the titans".

Brigadier Gerard won a vintage Guineas by three lengths from MILL REEF, with My Swallow a further three-quarters of a length back in third place. Paul Mellon's colt started favourite at Newmarket but, racing over a distance short of his best, he attempted to match strides with the speedy My Swallow, the pair effectively cutting each other's throats, allowing Brigadier Gerard to pounce inside the final furlong.

Ian Balding had mapped out a detailed programme for his little champion at the start of the season. After the Guineas his next target was to be the Epsom Derby. Ridden as usual by Welshman Geoff Lewis, MILL REEF easily justified favouritism at Epsom, coming with an irresistible run to lead at the furlong pole before pulling away to win by two lengths from Linden Tree, with Irish Ball back in third.

The golden run continued in the Eclipse Stakes. MILL REEF destroyed the top-class French four-year-old Caro by four effortless lengths at Sandown, demolishing the course record in the process. With Brigadier Gerard being trained for the major mile races, MILL REEF appeared to have the King George at his mercy.

MILL REEF faced nine opponents at Ascot. From France came the three-year-olds Acclimatization and Irish Ball, and the four-year-old Stintino. Of the three, Irish Ball appeared to have the best chance of upsetting the favourite. After winning the Prix Daru by one and a half lengths from Acclimatization, Irish Ball was a fast finishing fourth in the Epsom Derby, beaten by four and a half lengths by MILL REEF. That promise was fulfilled next time out when the son of Baldric II took advantage of MILL REEF's absence to land the Irish Sweeps Derby at the Curragh. Although he had over four lengths to make up on the Epsom form, Irish Ball appeared to be improving fast and was sent off the 9–2 second favourite at Ascot.

The Irish mounted a two-pronged challenge with Nor and Guillemot. Nor, who had been fourth in Nijinsky's Irish Sweeps Derby, was very much the second string at 500–1. Guillemot, who had run fourth in the Irish Two Thousand Guineas and third in the Irish Sweeps Derby, was the more fancied of the two, although only an optimist would have taken the 40–1 on offer.

A far more serious contender was the ex-Italian-trained Ortis.

Winner of the Italian Derby in 1970, the striking chestnut had joined Peter Walwyn in December of that year. On his first run for his new stable, Ortis, conceding five pounds to his opponent, went down by a neck to Pembroke Castle in the Coronation Stakes. After an easy victory in the Player Wills Stakes at Leopardstown, the four-year-old gained his revenge on Pembroke Castle with an emphatic eight-length win in the Hardwicke Stakes.

The Murless-Piggott representative, Politico, had been a useful three-year-old with a third place in the 1970 St Leger to his credit. Unfortunately, the son of Right Royal V had proved difficult to train and appeared to have little chance of reaching the frame. The remaining two runners, Bright Beam and Loud, were stable companions of MILL REEF and Ortis respectively, and were to act as pacemakers for the two principals.

MILL REEF gave his supporters one or two anxious moments during the preliminaries, uncharacteristically getting rather fractious. Lewis, quite sensibly, decided to risk the wrath of the stewards by taking his mount down to the start without parading in front of the stands.

Bouncing their mounts out of the stalls, Carter and Taylor set a strong gallop on the two pacemakers. The rest of the field were tucked in behind in a bunch, with the exception of Stintino who trailed the others by four or five lengths for the first six furlongs.

The writing was on the wall a long way from home. As the two pacemakers fell away with half a mile to run, MILL REEF was cantering in third place behind Politico and Ortis. As Piggott's mount weakened, Lewis eased MILL REEF alongside the hard-ridden Ortis. Cruising into the lead on the bridle at the distance, MILL REEF sauntered away from his rival with Lewis barely moving a muscle. Paul Mellon's black and yellow colours passed the post six lengths clear of Ortis, the widest winning margin since the race was introduced in 1951.

Acclimatization did best of the French trio, finishing a tired third, a short head in front of Stintino, who had come from an impossible position turning for home. After the race it transpired that the Boutin horse was lame in his near hind. Irish Ball was a major disappointment. At no stage of the race did the Irish Sweeps Derby winner appear to be going well, eventually finishing a poor fifth.

MILL REEF went to Longchamp the odds-on favourite to become

the first English-trained winner of the Prix de l'Arc de Triomphe since Migoli in 1948. That confidence was fully justified. A three-length victory over Pistol Packer in a new course record placed MILL REEF amongst the all time greats.

Unlike most modern Derby winners, MILL REEF remained in training as a four-year-old, with the King George and the Arc as his targets. The racing world eagerly awaited another clash between "the little horse" and "the Brigadier", who had remained unbeaten during 1971.

Everything appeared to be going to plan when MILL REEF won his first two races of 1972, the Prix Ganay and the Coronation Cup. MILL REEF then fell victim to a virus which prevented him taking on Brigadier Gerard in the King George.

Although he took a long time to recover, MILL REEF was back on course to run in the Arc when disaster struck. On August 30th horse-lovers all over the world were shocked to learn that MILL REEF had shattered his near fore during work on the Kingsclere gallops.

Thanks to skilled veterinary treatment and a six-hour operation, during which a steel plate was inserted into the leg, MILL REEF was able to take up stallion duties at the National Stud.

Winner of twelve of his fourteen races, worth £300,422, MILL REEF achieved glittering success as a stallion. Among his most illustrious offspring are the 1978 Derby winner Shirley Heights, the 1987 Derby winner Reference Point and the 1978 French Derby winner Acamas.

It came as a great blow to the British bloodstock industry when MILL REEF died at the age of eighteen on February 2nd, 1986.

# 1971

## KING GEORGE VI AND QUEEN ELIZABETH STAKES
## (GROUP ONE)

£31,558      1m 4f

July 24, 1971

| | | | |
|---|---|---|---|
| 1 MILL REEF (USA) | 3 | 8–7 | G. Lewis. b.c. by Never Bend–Milan Mill |
| 2 ORTIS (ITY) | 4 | 9–7 | D. Keith. ch.c. by Tissot–Orientale |
| 3 ACCLIMATIZATION (USA) (b) | 3 | 8–7 | J. C. Desaint. b.c. by Clem–Lola Montes |
| 4 STINTINO | 4 | 9–7 | A. Barclay. b.c. by Sheshoon–Cynara |
| 5 IRISH BALL (FR) | 3 | 8–7 | A. Gilbert. b.c. by Baldric II–Irish Lass |
| 6 POLITICO (USA) | 4 | 9–7 | L. Piggott. b.c. by Right Royal V–Tendentious |
| 7 GUILLEMOT (USA) | 3 | 8–7 | J. Mercer. b.c. by Sea Bird II–Belle Jeep |
| 8 NOR (b) | 4 | 9–7 | R. Parnell. b.c. by Tiger–Lucky Day |
| 9 BRIGHT BEAM (b) | 4 | 9–7 | T. Carter. ch.c. by Hornbeam–Golden Wedding |
| 10 LOUD (ITY) | 5 | 9–7 | B. Taylor. b.h. by Silver Cloud–Licence |

10 Ran

Going – Good

Distances: 61,31,sht hd,61,21

Time: 2:32.56

S.P. 8–13 MILL REEF, 9–2 IRISH BALL, 11–1 ORTIS, 14–1 POLITICO, STINTINO, 35–1 GUILLEMOT, 40–1 ACCLIMATIZATION, 100–1 NOR, 500–1 OTHERS

Winner trained by I. Balding at Kingsclere: owned by Mr P. Mellon: bred by Rokeby Farm, Virginia

Timeform rating of winner 141

# 1972

 ew racehorses deserve the epithet "great" but when used to
describe BRIGADIER GERARD, the word is sadly inadequate.
Although he achieved victory in the mile and a half King
George, BRIGADIER GERARD will forever be remembered as one of the
most outstanding milers of all time.

Bred by his owners, John and Jean Hislop, the son of Queen's
Hussar was named after the character created by Arthur Conan
Doyle in *The Exploits of Brigadier Gerard*. His sire, despite victories in
the Lockinge Stakes and the Sussex Stakes, was very much an
unfashionable stallion when he visited the Prince Chevalier mare La
Paiva, but the resultant foal developed into a splendid mahogany
bay, with black points and a small white star.

John Hislop, a former champion amateur jockey and universally
respected journalist, belonged to the old school of owner-breeders.
Before BRIGADIER GERARD had ever set foot on a racecourse, the
Hislops decided that the colt would never be sold at any price.

Although never spectacular on the West Ilsey gallops, BRIGADIER
GERARD made an immediate impression on his trainer Major Hern.
Throughout his career the colt took delight in depositing his work
riders on the Berkshire turf, even stable jockey Joe Mercer was given
"the treatment".

After winning all four of his races as a two-year-old, culminating in
a three-length victory over Mummy's Pet in the Middle Park Stakes,
BRIGADIER GERARD was allotted nine stone, five pounds in the Free
Handicap, two pounds behind the top-rated colt Mill Reef, and one
pound behind My Swallow.

A vintage crop of three-year-olds did battle in 1971. The Two
Thousand Guineas field was the strongest for years, with Mill Reef
and My Swallow taking on the BRIGADIER. Without the benefit of a

preparatory race, BRIGADIER GERARD put up a sparkling performance to beat Mill Reef by three-quarters of a length. Major Hern would later repeat this marvellous feat of training with Nashwan in 1989.

After the Guineas the racing public eagerly awaited another clash between BRIGADIER GERARD and Mill Reef, but, although both horses remained in training as four-year-olds, the rematch never took place. While Mill Reef was probably the better horse over twelve furlongs, BRIGADIER GERARD was undoubtedly the superior miler.

BRIGADIER GERARD ended his second season undefeated. After the Two Thousand Guineas he recorded victories in the St James's Palace Stakes, the Sussex Stakes, the Goodwood Mile, the Queen Elizabeth II Stakes and the Champion Stakes. Together with his regular partner, Joe Mercer, he achieved a sequence of ten consecutive wins.

After the Champion Stakes, the Hislops made the decision to keep the colt in training as a four-year-old, assuming they would never be fortunate enough to own a horse of such ability again.

The horse looked magnificent after his winter break and continued his winning sequence in the Lockinge Stakes, beating Grey Mirage by two and a half lengths. After easily winning the Westbury Stakes at Sandown, BRIGADIER GERARD recorded one of his best performances in beating Steel Pulse by an effortless five lengths in the Prince of Wales Stakes at Royal Ascot. The form was made to look cast iron when Steel Pulse went on to land the Irish Sweeps Derby.

Following such a magnificent display at Royal Ascot, it came as a disappointment when in his next race, the Eclipse Stakes, BRIGADIER GERARD struggled to beat Gold Rod by a length in soft ground. After the race, John Hislop announced that his colt would never be asked to race on such going again.

As a three-year-old, BRIGADIER GERARD had not contested the Derby because his connections believed he would not get the trip. Those doubts to some extent still existed when the decision was made to go for the King George. The prestige of the Ascot race was such, that John Hislop and Major Hern decided to take a positive attitude. With his relaxed style of racing and the physical improvement he had made from three to four, there was every chance that the BRIGADIER would be capable of stepping up to a mile and a half.

BRIGADIER GERARD lined up at Ascot unbeaten in fourteen races, a fact reflected in the starting price, 8–13. In addition to tackling a mile and a half for the first time, the BRIGADIER had to face opposition of the highest calibre. Although Mill Reef was injured and therefore unable to attempt a King George double, the race had, as usual, attracted top-class candidates.

From France came the handsome Never Bend colt Riverman. Winner of the Poule d'Essai des Poulains, the Prix Jean Prat and the Prix d'Ispahan already in 1972, the three-year-old seemed a formidable rival for "the Brigadier". The Italian representative, Gay Lussac, was a big lanky chestnut with lop ears. Lester Piggott's mount had won all seven of his previous races, including the Derby Italiano. Newmarket hopes rested with the four-year-old Parnell. Winner of the 1971 Irish St Leger, the St Paddy colt was guaranteed to stay every yard of the trip. The Irish Sweeps Derby winner, Steel Pulse, appeared to have little chance of finishing in front of BRIGADIER GERARD on their running in the Prince of Wales Stakes, where Major Hern's horse had five lengths to spare.

A fine day, and the presence of the BRIGADIER, attracted a huge crowd to Ascot for the twenty-second running of the King George, sponsored for the first time by De Beers Consolidated Mines Ltd. Down at the start, two horses stood out from their rivals – Riverman and BRIGADIER GERARD. Both looked in superb condition, ready to run for their lives.

It is essential at Ascot to be on the heels of the leaders turning into the short straight and so Major Hern told Joe Mercer to ride BRIGADIER GERARD "under the assumption that the horse stays"; in other words, to keep him handy throughout.

Selhurst, carrying the famous red and black Jim Joel colours, was the first to show, closely followed by Parnell, Sukawa, Gay Lussac and Steel Pulse. Mercer had BRIGADIER GERARD nicely placed in behind the leading bunch. At the rear of the field, Freddie Head held up Riverman for a late run.

After five furlongs, Willie Carson kicked Parnell into the lead, quickening the pace in an attempt to test BRIGADIER GERARD's stamina to the full. Turning into the straight, the race had developed into a match between Parnell and "the Brigadier".

With Carson pumping away, Parnell still held a two-length advantage with two furlongs to run. Agonisingly slowly, BRIGADIER GERARD began to inch closer to his rival. Sheer class took him into the lead just over a furlong out. At this point Mercer felt his mount drift right towards the hard-ridden Parnell. The wily Carson stood up in his irons in order to exaggerate the effect of the deviation before switching his mount to the outside of BRIGADIER GERARD.

As the noise from the packed grandstand reached a crescendo, BRIGADIER GERARD forged a length and a half clear of Parnell to record an historic victory. Riverman, who had trailed the field for much of the race, made up a tremendous amount of ground to take third place, five lengths behind Parnell.

A Stewards' inquiry was inevitably announced. Carson was sure he would be awarded the race, but the head-on recording clearly showed that the interference had been both accidental and slight. In addition, the Stewards also found that Parnell himself had deviated from a straight course and consequently allowed the result to stand.

Although he won the race, the King George proved that BRIGADIER GERARD did not truly stay a mile and a half – it was only a combination of class and courage that allowed him to hold off the dour stayer Parnell inside the final furlong.

BRIGADIER GERARD raced on two further occasions after Ascot, and the entire racing world was plunged into a state of shock when the BRIGADIER lost his unbeaten record in the Benson and Hedges Gold Cup at York. Sent off the 3–1 on favourite, he could never quite catch the Epsom Derby winner Roberto who made all in the hands of Panamanian Braulio Baeza to record a three-length victory. BRIGADIER GERARD fought his final battle in the Champion Stakes where he accounted for his old rival Riverman by one and a half lengths.

The Hislops sold twenty-four shares in BRIGADIER GERARD to private breeders, retaining overall control of the horse's future themselves. "The Brigadier" retired to Egerton Stud, the place of his birth, the winner of seventeen of his eighteen races. Successful in Group One races over distances from six furlongs to a mile and a half, BRIGADIER GERARD was rated at 144 by Timeform, a figure bettered only by Sea Bird II.

Despite his unfashionable pedigree, great things were expected of BRIGADIER GERARD as a stallion. Yet it must be said that his progeny have proved somewhat disappointing with the exception of the 1980 St Leger winner Light Cavalry, the 1981 Champion Stakes winner Vayrann and the 1978 Champagne Stakes winner R. B. Chesne. Sadly for his many admirers, BRIGADIER GERARD died of a heart attack in October 1989.

# 1972

## KING GEORGE VI AND QUEEN ELIZABETH STAKES
## (GROUP ONE)

£60,202     1m 4f

July 22, 1972

| | | | |
|---|---|---|---|
| 1 BRIGADIER GERARD | 4 | 9–7 | J. Mercer. b.c. by Queen's Hussar–La Paiva |
| 2 PARNELL | 4 | 9–7 | W. Carson. ch.c. by St Paddy–Nella |
| 3 RIVERMAN (USA) | 3 | 8–7 | F. Head. b.c. by Never Bend–River Lady |
| 4 STEEL PULSE | 3 | 8–7 | W. Williamson. br.c. by Diatome–Rachel |
| 5 GAY LUSSAC (ITY) | 3 | 8–7 | L. Piggott. ch.c. by Faberge II–Green as Grass |
| 6 BOG ROAD | 3 | 8–7 | J. Lindley. b.c. by Busted–Royal Danseuse |
| 7 SUKAWA (FR) | 3 | 8–7 | Y. Saint Martin. br.c. by Sodium–Serge de Nimes |
| 8 SELHURST | 4 | 9–7 | G. Lewis. b.c. by Charlottesville–Crystal Palace |
| 9 FAIR WORLD | 4 | 9–7 | F. Durr. b.c. by Worden II–Fair Share |

9 Ran

Going – Good

Distances: 1½,5,2,1,2

Time: 2:32.91

S.P. 8–13 BRIGADIER GERARD, 5–1 GAY LUSSAC, 17–2 RIVERMAN, 12–1 SELHURST, 14–1 STEEL PULSE, 28–1 PARNELL, SUKAWA, 66–1 OTHERS

Winner trained by Major Hern at West Ilsley: owned by Mr J. Hislop: bred by owner

Timeform rating of winner 144

# 1973

DAHLIA, the 1973 King George heroine, was one of the toughest fillies of the post-war era. Bred by her larger than life owner, the American oil tycoon Nelson Bunker Hunt, she was from the first crop of Vaguely Noble, out of the Honest Alibi mare Charming Alibi.

Although she belonged to the same generation as the brilliant Allez France, DAHLIA made a lasting impression on the international racing scene. As a two-year-old, DAHLIA was rated seven pounds behind Allez France, having scored just one victory from four outings.

It was, however, as a three-year-old that the chestnut filly really began to bloom. After winning the Prix de la Grotte over a mile at Longchamp, DAHLIA was beaten into third place by Allez France and Princess Arjumand in the Poule d'Essai des Pouliches. This was the first of six occasions on which Bunker Hunt's filly was beaten by Allez France – indeed, throughout her illustrious career DAHLIA never managed to beat her great rival.

Stepping up to ten furlongs, DAHLIA returned to winning ways in the Prix Saint Alary, coming home one and a half lengths clear of Virunga. This victory was, however, followed by another defeat by Allez France, this time in the Prix de Diane.

In order to escape the formidable shadow of her great rival, Zilber sent DAHLIA to contest the Irish Guinness Oaks at the Curragh. Starting second favourite at 8–1, the daughter of Vaguely Noble ran a magnificent race to snatch the prize from the previously unbeaten One Thousand Guineas and Oaks winner Mysterious. Seven days after her Curragh triumph, Zilber sent DAHLIA to Ascot for the King George. The only filly in a field of twelve, DAHLIA faced opposition of the highest calibre.

Despite DAHLIA's splendid victory in Ireland, most observers considered the King George to be a two-way contest between the four-year-olds Roberto and Rheingold. Roberto had already achieved immortality on two counts, firstly by snatching the 1972 Epsom Derby under an inspired ride from Piggott, and secondly by becoming the only horse ever to defeat the mighty Brigadier Gerard, a feat achieved in the 1972 Benson and Hedges Gold Cup at York.

Roberto began his 1973 campaign in the Nijinsky Stakes at Leopardstown where, after a titanic struggle, he went down by three-quarters of a length to Ballymore. Returning to the scene of his Derby triumph, the son of Hail to Reason next added the Coronation Cup to his list of Group race victories, with an emphatic five-length win over Attica Meli. O'Brien had hoped to run Roberto in the Eclipse Stakes which was run at Kempton, due to building reconstruction at Sandown. Unfortunately soft going prevented his participation. The good ground at Ascot would pose no such problems and Roberto was sent off the 3–1 second favourite.

The Barry Hills-trained Rheingold was made favourite on the day. The 1972 Derby runner-up boasted four consecutive victories prior to the King George. After taking Newbury's John Porter Stakes on his seasonal reappearance, Rheingold went on to land the Prix Ganay, the Hardwicke Stakes, and the Grand Prix de Saint-Cloud, partnered on each occasion by the French champion Yves Saint-Martin.

Of the remainder, Parnell, second to Brigadier Gerard in 1972, and Scottish Rifle, winner of four of his five races in 1973, appeared to hold the best credentials.

Park Lawn, pacemaker for the Irish Sweeps Derby winner Weaver's Hall, cut out the early running, closely followed by his stable companion and Roberto. At the five furlong marker Piggott pushed Roberto into a clear lead in an effort to steal the race. Turning into the straight, Roberto still led from Weaver's Hall, Hard to Beat and Scottish Rifle with the rest of the field, with the exception of the weakening Park Lawn, grouped in behind.

Three furlongs out Bill Pyers made his move on DAHLIA, making rapid headway from the rear of the field. As Roberto surprisingly weakened, the filly hit the front, slightly hampering the hard-ridden Parnell in the process. With an amazing burst of acceleration, DAHLIA opened up a six-length lead over the fast-finishing

Rheingold, thus equalling Mill Reef's record-winning distance. The Frank Durr-ridden Our Mirage put up the best performance of his career to take third place. The major disappointment of the race was undoubtedly Roberto who finished eleventh of the twelve runners.

DAHLIA, the first three-year-old filly to win the King George, ran in the Prix Vermeille and the Prix de l'Arc de Triomphe after Ascot, finding Allez France again too good for her, both fillies finishing behind Rheingold in the latter race. She did, however, end her season in a blaze of glory by becoming the first filly to win the Washington International since its inception in 1952. After her American victory, Bunker Hunt announced that DAHLIA would remain in training as a four-year-old, with the King George as one of her main targets. No horse had ever won Ascot's showpiece twice. Could the daughter of Vaguely Noble retain her crown in 1974?

# 1973

## KING GEORGE VI AND QUEEN ELIZABETH STAKES (GROUP ONE)

£79,230     1m 4f

July 28, 1973

| | | | |
|---|---|---|---|
| 1 DAHLIA (USA) | 3 8–4 | W. Pyers. ch.f. by Vaguely Noble–Charming Alibi |
| 2 RHEINGOLD | 4 9–7 | Y. Saint-Martin. b.c. by Faberge II–Athene |
| 3 OUR MIRAGE | 4 9–7 | F. Durr. ch.c. by Miralgo–Ardent Range |
| 4 WEAVER'S HALL | 3 8–7 | G. McGrath. b.c. by Busted–Marians |
| 5 PARNELL | 5 9–7 | W. Carson. ch.h. by St Paddy–Nella |
| 6 CARD KING (USA) | 5 9–7 | A. Murray. br.h. by Cardington King–Nautua II |
| 7 SCOTTISH RIFLE | 4 9–7 | R. Hutchinson. bl.c. by Sunny Way–Radiopye |
| 8 KLAIRVIMY | 3 8–7 | R. Parnell. ch.c. by Klairon–Vimy Line |
| 9 HARD TO BEAT | 4 9–7 | J. Lindley. b.c. by Hardicanute–Virtuous |
| 10 YAROSLAV | 4 9–7 | G. Lewis. ch.c. by Santa Claus–Bleu Azur |
| 11 ROBERTO (USA) | 4 9–7 | L. Piggott. b.c. by Hail to Reason–Bramalea |
| 12 PARK LAWN | 3 8–7 | P. Eddery. ch.c. by Lauso–Nellie Park |

12 Ran

Going – Good

Distances: 6l,2l,nk,nk,½l,2l

Time: 2:30.43

S.P. 13–8 RHEINGOLD, 3–1 ROBERTO, 10–1 DAHLIA, PARNELL, 14–1 SCOTTISH RIFLE, YAROSLAV, WEAVER'S HALL, 16–1 HARD TO BEAT, 25–1 OUR MIRAGE, 50–1 KLAIRVIMY, 100–1 CARD KING, 200–1 PARK LAWN

Winner trained by Maurice Zilber at Chantilly: owned by Mr N. Bunker Hunt: bred by owner in USA

Timeform rating of winner 132

# 1974

DAHLIA returned to Ascot in 1974, the 15–8 favourite to pull off an unprecedented second victory.

The Vaguely Noble filly had started her four-year-old campaign in an all too familiar way, chasing home her old rival Allez France in the Prix d'Harcourt and the Prix Ganay. After running a respectable third behind Buoy and Tennyson in the Coronation Cup, the filly scored her first victory of the season in the Grand Prix de Saint-Cloud, where she was ridden by Yves Saint-Martin in place of the out of favour Pyers. Lester Piggott, who had ridden DAHLIA as a two-year-old, was reunited with the filly at Ascot.

On paper DAHLIA faced an easier task than she had done the previous year. Of her nine opponents, only four were seriously considered to be in with a chance and the most dangerous of them appeared to be the Queen's Highclere. A daughter of Queen's Hussar, she was unbeaten as a three-year-old prior to Ascot, and as the first filly ever to land the One Thousand Guineas–Prix Diane double, Highclere seemed to have a fine chance of becoming the second royal King George winner.

The Marcel Boussac-owned Dankaro was another with sound credentials. Successful in the Prix Greffulhe and the Prix Lupin, the son of Dan Cupid had run a splendid race to finish runner-up to Caracolero in the Prix du Jockey Club.

Snow Knight, the surprise 50–1 Derby winner, would need to improve considerably in order to trouble the likes of DAHLIA and Highclere. Brian Taylor had "stolen" the race at Epsom, building up a decisive lead on the descent to Tattenham Corner. With Hippodamia in the field to ensure a strong pace for DAHLIA, Taylor would have his work cut out to steal the King George in a similar fashion.

In addition to Highclere, Dick Hern was represented by the four-year-old Buoy. The imposing chestnut already boasted a victory over DAHLIA, having beaten the filly by a comfortable four and a half lengths in the Coronation Cup. However, Zilber was characteristically confident of reversing the positions at Ascot, arguing that his filly always took time to reach peak form. With a month's sun on her back she would be a different proposition in the King George.

The Italian raider Orsa Maggiore was an interesting runner. Winner of the Oaks d'Italia in 1973, she arrived at Ascot unbeaten as a four-year-old, having won all her four races, culminating in a half-length victory over Sang Bleu in the Gran Premio di Milano in June.

The remainder, the six-year-old Card King and the four-year-olds Conor Pass and Freefoot appeared to be out of their depth.

The omens appeared good for the DAHLIA camp when Piggott won the two races prior to the King George on Olympic Casino and Roussalka. Dankaro was easily the pick of the paddock, although the lightly made DAHLIA looked trained to the minute with not an ounce of extraneous flesh in evidence. DAHLIA's pacemaker Hippodamia was a high-class filly in her own right, having run Dumka to a length in the 1974 Poule d'Essai des Pouliches. In the event she carried out her duties to the letter. Taking the lead from the break, Hippodamia set a searching pace for nine and a half furlongs. Only on the turn into the straight did she begin to weaken, allowing Snow Knight and Buoy to take up the running.

With two furlongs to run Snow Knight held the lead from Buoy, Highclere, DAHLIA and Dankaro. The writing was on the wall from the furlong marker. As Piggott let out an inch of rein on his filly the response was electric. Still on the bit, DAHLIA cruised past her toiling rivals as if they were standing still. At the post Bunker Hunt's filly had two and a half lengths to spare over Highclere with Dankaro a further length back in third.

DAHLIA had become the first dual winner of the King George. But her season was far from over.

In a glorious sequence, DAHLIA recorded scintillating victories in the Benson and Hedges Gold Cup, the Man o'War Stakes and the Canadian International Championship Stakes to earn the "Racehorse of the Year" title for the second time.

Like her dam, the veteran of seventy-one races, DAHLIA thrived on racing and remained in training as a five-year-old, adding a second Benson and Hedges Gold Cup to her impressive list of Group race victories.

In 1976 DAHLIA returned to her native America where, under the care of the legendary Charlie Whittingham, she won two races at Hollywood Park before retiring to stud in Kentucky. Unlike her great rival Allez France, she made a successful transition from race mare to brood mare. Among her Group-winning offspring are Dahar and Rivlia.

Seldom has a filly shown the toughness and enthusiasm for racing exhibited by DAHLIA throughout her long and illustrious career. She was always a credit to her connections.

# 1974

## KING GEORGE VI AND QUEEN ELIZABETH STAKES
### (GROUP ONE)

£81,240     1m 4f

July 27, 1974

| | | | |
|---|---|---|---|
| 1 DAHLIA (USA) | 4 | 9–4 | L. Piggott. ch.f. by Vaguely Noble–Charming Alibi |
| 2 HIGHCLERE | 3 | 8–4 | J. Mercer. b.f. by Queen's Hussar–Highlight |
| 3 DANKARO (FR) | 3 | 8–7 | G. Rivases. ch.c. by Dan Cupid–Takaroa |
| 4 BUOY | 4 | 9–7 | J. Lindley. ch.c. by Aureole–Ripeck |
| 5 CARD KING (USA) | 6 | 9–7 | W. Pyers. br.h. by Cardington King–Nantua II |
| 6 SNOW KNIGHT | 3 | 8–7 | B. Taylor. ch.c. by Firestreak–Snow Blossom |
| 7 ORSA MAGGIORE | 4 | 9–4 | G. Dettori. b.f. by Ruysdael II–Oliveira |
| 8 FREEFOOT | 4 | 9–7 | G. Starkey. b.c. by Relko–Close Up |
| 9 HIPPODAMIA (USA) | 3 | 8–4 | Peter Cook, br.f. by Hail to Reason–White Lie |
| 10 CONOR PASS | 4 | 9–7 | P. Jarman. br.c. by Tiepolo II–Windfield Lily |

10 Ran

Going – Good

Distances: 2½,1,2,½,3,nk,1

Time: 2:33.03

S.P. 15–8 DAHLIA, 5–1 HIGHCLERE, 11–2 SNOW KNIGHT, 6–1 DANKARO, 7–1 BUOY, 20–1 ORSA MAGGIORE, 25–1 CARD KING, 33–1 HIPPODAMIA, 66–1 OTHERS

Winner trained in France by M. Zilber: owned by Mr N. Bunker Hunt: bred by owner in USA

Timeform rating of winner 135

# 1975

Although De Beers had sponsored the King George since 1972, the now familiar title, "The King George VI and Queen Elizabeth Diamond Stakes", did not appear until 1975. The first "run for the Diamonds" was to produce what is generally known as the greatest race ever.

The 1975 line-up was an impressive gathering of equine talent. Dahlia, heroine in 1973 and 1974 was seeking a hat trick, and she spearheaded a strong French challenge. Although the mare had finished unplaced in each of her four runs prior to Ascot, she had shown a glimmer of her former brilliance when fifth to Un Kopeck at Saint-Cloud on her previous outing. The other French raiders, Ashmore, Card King, and On My Way were all capable of taking the £81,910 prize across the English Channel if they hit top form. The Germans were also optimistic. Their representative, Star Appeal, had proved himself a performer of the highest class with victories in the Eclipse Stakes and the Gran Premio Milano.

However, despite the impressive qualifications of the foreign raiders, attention had been focused in the weeks leading up to the race almost entirely on the eagerly awaited clash between the champion three-year-old GRUNDY and the outstanding four-year-old Bustino.

For more than a decade Lady Beaverbrook had been one of the most ardent supporters of British racing. Yet, until Bustino provided a first Classic success in the 1974 St Leger, her massive capital outlay had yielded scant reward.

Like the majority of Busted's offspring, Bustino needed time to show his full potential. The 21,000 guineas purchase was given just a single outing as a two-year-old, in the Acomb Stakes at York, where he finished a promising third. The following season he won both the

Sandown Classic Trial and the Ladbroke Derby Trial, beating Snow Knight on both occasions. He then found the going too firm at Epsom but still managed to finish fourth behind his old rival Snow Knight. After finishing second in the Grand Prix de Paris, Bustino ended his three-year-old season in a blaze of glory winning the Great Voltigeur Stakes and the St Leger.

Bustino developed into a most imposing four-year-old. On his only outing prior to the King George he smashed the Epsom mile and a half course record when toying with the opposition in the Coronation Cup. His connections set their sights firmly on the big Ascot prize.

GRUNDY was a member of an increasingly exclusive club, a Derby winner purchased as a yearling at public auction. Bought by blood-stock agent Keith Freeman for 11,000 guineas on behalf of Italian industrialist Dr Carlo Vittadini at the 1973 Newmarket October Sales, GRUNDY was put into training with Peter Walwyn at Lambourn.

The flashy chestnut with the three white feet and the distinctive jagged blaze boasted a pedigree which combined speed and stamina. His sire, Great Nephew, had been a high-class performer, winning the Prix du Moulin de Longchamp and the Prix Dollar in addition to running second in both the Two Thousand Guineas and the Eclipse. From his dam, Word From Lundy, a daughter of Worden II, GRUNDY inherited the stamina which would prove so decisive during his racing career.

Unlike the slow-maturing Bustino, GRUNDY was a precocious two-year-old, heading the Free Handicap after winning all four of his juvenile races, culminating in an impressive victory in the Dewhurst Stakes at Newmarket.

After suffering a shock defeat by Mark Anthony in the Greenham Stakes on his seasonal reappearance, GRUNDY ran a courageous second to Bolkonski in the Two Thousand Guineas despite still suffering the effects of a kick from a stable companion on the Lambourn gallops. The little chestnut soon returned to winning ways, storming away with the Irish Two Thousand Guineas at the Curragh. Despite this victory GRUNDY did not head the market for the Derby, in which the French-trained Green Dancer started favourite. In the event the Gallic raider never looked like winning as GRUNDY produced blinding acceleration in the final furlong to beat the filly Nobiliary by an effortless three lengths. Next came the Irish Sweeps Derby and a two-length win over King Pellinore.

And so to Ascot for the King George, where the stage was set, for the champion three-year-old to do battle with his elders for the first time.

Expectant racegoers flocked to the Berkshire course in their thousands. Motorists were forced to sit and suffer in the sweltering heat as they inched their way towards the course. Not a drop of rain had fallen for weeks, so the going would be firm despite extensive watering. The feeling amongst the racing press was that Bustino would be better suited to the fast conditions, yet the weight of money was for GRUNDY who was backed down to 4–5, with Bustino on offer at 4–1, and the hat trick-seeking Dahlia on the 6–1 mark.

Peter Walwyn had twice previously saddled the runner-up in the big race, Crozier in 1969 and Ortis in 1971. Was he about to go one better with GRUNDY? The afternoon began full of promise for the Walwyn camp, with Dr Vittadini's daughter Franca winning the ladies' Star of Sierra Leone Diamond Stakes on Hard Day. The omens looked auspicious.

In the rival camp Bustino's connections had drawn up a detailed battle strategy which, they hoped, would enable their four-year-old to outpoint his rivals. Bustino would have the benefit of two pace-makers in an attempt to blunt GRUNDY's blinding finishing speed. Trainer Dick Hern and jockey Joe Mercer were determined that the race should be a true test of stamina from the off. Hern had planned to run Riboson as a pacemaker, but unfortunately the horse suffered a cracked cannon bone, and the task of running the heart out of GRUNDY fell to the five-year-old Kinglet and the three-year-old Highest. Kinglet was to be ridden by Eric Eldin and Highest by Frankie Durr.

In the parade ring both GRUNDY and Bustino looked magnificent, as did the 1974 Irish Oaks winner Dibidale. Down at the start the German-trained Star Appeal was easy to spot with his distinctive green blinkers. Dahlia was also conspicuous but for the wrong reasons. The mare was giving the handlers a hard time before eventually consenting to enter the stalls.

Surprisingly Bustino was the first to show from the break. Highest, drawn one on the outside, had to come across the whole field in order to get to the rails position. Once he found the rails Durr kicked on followed closely by Kinglet, Star Appeal, Bustino and GRUNDY. The pace seemed suicidal and after two furlongs the field had stretched out in Indian file. After four and a half furlongs Highest had reached the limit of his resources and rapidly lost his place. At this point the second stage of Dick Hern's plan was put into operation as Eldin drove Kinglet into the lead.

Turning into Swinley Bottom, the two principals were going extremely well in behind Kinglet and Star Appeal. At the half-mile pole Mercer sensed that Kinglet had come to the end of his tether, and in an instant kicked Bustino into the lead. Eddery had been watching Mercer like a hawk and now urged his horse to go after the four-year-old. The response was not immediate, and as they turned into the straight Bustino had the advantage by four lengths. What happened next over Ascot's three-furlong straight will forever remain ingrained in the memories of those fortunate enough to have been part of the seething gallery in the grandstands.

GRUNDY, under the strongest driving from Eddery, passed Star Appeal and began to make up the leeway on Bustino. Two furlongs out Bustino still had three lengths to spare. GRUNDY responded to two cracks of Eddery's whip to claw his way level with the older horse's quarters. With a furlong to run they were level and the war of attrition was about to reach its climax.

Mercer, the supreme stylist, drove out Bustino in his inimitable hands and heels fashion. Again and again Eddery's stick came down as GRUNDY inched ahead fifty yards from the line. Bustino fought back bravely, but the three-year-old just had it. The roar from the crowd as GRUNDY passed the post a half-length clear of his rival was awesome. Both horses were visibly heaving and shaking with exhaustion as their pilots eased them to a walk. Hardened racegoers were openly in tears. Both horses were greeted as heroes.

GRUNDY had had his stamina and courage tested to the limit and responded magnificently. Bustino had run the race of his life, failing by only half a length to give fourteen pounds to the best three-year-old in Europe. Dahlia too, although failing to complete a unique hat trick, had run a splendid race to finish third.

GRUNDY's winning time of 2:26.98 seconds smashed Dahlia's previous course record by a remarkable 2.36 seconds, making it the fastest mile and a half ever electrically recorded in Britain. Even Ashmore placed sixth had beaten the old record. Once again the

King George had provided a magnificent test for the thoroughbred racehorse.

1975 proved to be an outstanding year for GRUNDY's connections. Peter Walwyn finished the season as Champion Trainer and, at the age of twenty-three, Pat Eddery became the youngest Champion Jockey for fifty years. Great Nephew was Leading Sire, and Dr Vittadini was voted Owner of the Year.

GRUNDY's final racecourse appearance came in the Benson and Hedges Gold Cup at York where he ran below form to finish fourth to a rejuvenated Dahlia. He retired the winner of eight of his eleven races, with the total earnings of £326,421, at the time a record for a horse trained in England.

He began his stud career at the National Stud in Newmarket but was exported to Japan in 1983. GRUNDY's most successful representative to date is the 1980 Oaks winner Bireme.

After Ascot, Bustino was aimed at the Arc de Triomphe but developed an injury during his preparation. He never raced again. On all known form he had the Arc at his mercy, the winner Star Appeal having finished only ninth at Ascot. Bustino now stands at the Queen's Wolferton Stud in Norfolk.

# 1975

## KING GEORGE VI AND QUEEN ELIZABETH DIAMOND STAKES (GROUP ONE)

£81,910      1m 4f

July 26, 1975

| | | | |
|---|---|---|---|
| 1 GRUNDY | 3 | 8–7 | P. Eddery. ch.c. by Great Nephew–Word From Lundy |
| 2 BUSTINO | 4 | 9–7 | J. Mercer. b.c. by Busted–Ship Yard |
| 3 DAHLIA (USA) | 5 | 9–4 | L. Piggott. ch.m. by Vaguely Noble–Charming Alibi |
| 4 ON MY WAY (USA) | 5 | 9–7 | W. Pyers. b.h. by Laugh Aloud–Gracious Me |
| 5 CARD KING (USA) | 7 | 9–7 | R. Jaliu. br.h. by Cardington King–Nantua II |
| 6 ASHMORE | 4 | 9–7 | Y. Saint-Martin. b.c. by Lunthier–Almyre |
| 7 DIBIDALE | 4 | 9–4 | W. Carson. ch.f. by Aggressor–Priddy Maid |
| 8 LIBRA'S RIB (USA) | 3 | 8–7 | F. Morby. ch.c. by Ribot–Libra |
| 9 STAR APPEAL | 5 | 9–7 | G. Starkey. b.h. by Appiani II–Sterna |
| 10 KINGLET | 5 | 9–7 | E. Eldin. b.h. by Pampered King–War Ribbon |
| 11 HIGHEST | 3 | 8–7 | F. Durr. b.c. by Crepello–Highest Hopes |

11 Ran

Going – Firm

Distances: ½l,5l,1½l,½l,1½l,7l,4l,2½l

Time: 2:26.98

S.P. 4–5 GRUNDY, 4–1 BUSTINO, 6–1 DAHLIA, 13–1 STAR APPEAL, 18–1 ASH-MORE, 20–1 ON MY WAY, 33–1 DIBIDALE, LIBRA'S RIB, 66–1 CARD KING, 500–1 OTHERS

Winner trained by P. T. Walwyn at Seven Barrows, Lambourn: owned by Dr Carlo Vittadini: bred by Overbury Stud

Timeform rating of winner 137

# 1976

Prior to PAWNEESE's victory in 1976, only two horses had successfully made all the running in the King George – Match III in 1962, and Nasram II in 1964. Angel Penna's filly was vastly superior to the latter and at least the equal of the former.

The Penna-Wildenstein-Saint-Martin team had a spectacular season in 1976, landing three of the five English Classics. Flying Water, a delightful Habitat filly, took the One Thousand Guineas, PAWNEESE the Oaks, and Crow the St Leger.

After Flying Water had beaten Konafa in the One Thousand Guineas, her trainer astounded onlookers by announcing that he had a better filly at home. That filly was PAWNEESE.

A rather lightly built individual, her pedigree hardly promised Classic-winning ability. Until PAWNEESE, Carvin had sired little of note. Her dam, Plencia, had been a useful performer, winning two mile and a quarter races in France, but she was unproven as a broodmare. PAWNEESE was her first foal.

A natural frontrunner with a preference for top-of-the-ground conditions, PAWNEESE had been beaten in both of her races as a two-year-old. By the time she made her three-year-old debut in the Prix la Camago at Saint-Cloud, however, PAWNEESE was being hailed as the best filly in Penna's stable. Her trainer's confidence was fully justified, and she won the race unextended. Penna sent his filly back to Saint-Cloud for her next two races. After landing the Group III Prix Penelope, she beat a field of useful fillies in the Prix Cléopâtre, making all the running in the process.

With the stable's Flying Water the winner of the One Thousand Guineas, PAWNEESE was all the rage for the Oaks. Starting the 6–5 favourite, she made the rest of the field look ordinary, coming home five lengths clear of Roses For The Star.

Her next performance was just as impressive. PAWNEESE slaughtered a quality field of fillies in the Prix de Diane, and in beating Riverqueen by one and a half lengths, with the Irish One Thousand Guineas winner Sarah Siddons back in fifth place, Penna's filly earned her place in the King George line up. The Prix de Diane form was made to look ultra-reliable when Riverqueen beat older colts in the Grand Prix de Saint-Cloud, and Lagunette, who had been third at Chantilly, took the Irish Guinness Oaks.

Despite these brilliant performances, PAWNEESE did not start favourite at Ascot, her compatriot, Youth, being preferred. In a season dominated by French-trained horses, Youth arrived at Ascot unbeaten as a three-year-old, with four successive wins to his credit. A son of the versatile American sire Ack Ack, Youth started the 1976 season with easy victories over second-rate opponents in the Prix Greffulhe and the Prix Daru. On his third outing, he put up a most impressive performance, accounting for the top-class Arctic Tern and the future Epsom Derby winner, Empery, in the Prix Lupin. The victorious sequence continued in the Prix du Jockey Club. In beating Twig Moss and Malacate, the Maurice Zilber-trained colt laid claims to being the champion three-year-old of 1976.

Malacate, beaten three and three-quarter lengths at Chantilly, franked the form in no uncertain manner by destroying Empery in the Irish Sweeps Derby. After the race, trainer François Boutin announced that Malacate would renew rivalry with Youth in the King George. With PAWNEESE a certain runner, the French appeared to have the Ascot race at their mercy

The four-year-olds, Bruni and Orange Bay, appeared to provide the only realistic home-trained opposition to the French raiders. Bruni, runaway winner of the 1975 St Leger, had started the current season in promising fashion. Conceding weight to his four opponents, the grey had found little difficulty in accounting for Mr Bigmore by two lengths in the Yorkshire Cup. In his only other race prior to the King George, he had been beaten by a head by Orange Bay in the Hardwicke Stakes after losing ten lengths at the start. Connections were confident that the son of Sea Hawk II would gain revenge at Ascot.

As a three year old, Orange Bay had won the Italian Derby prior to joining Peter Walwyn. Owned, like Grundy, by Dr Carlo Vittadini, Orange Bay was one of the best-looking horses in training.

Prior to his victory in the Hardwicke Stakes, Pat Eddery's mount had beaten a useful field to win the Jockey Club Stakes at Newmarket.

Few observers gave the remaining participants–Coin of Gold, Record Run and Dakota for England, the Italian-trained Duke of Marmalade and the fourth French raider, Ashmore–more than a passing glance. The three English representatives were apparently only talented handicappers. Duke of Marmalade looked out of his depth while Ashmore, who had finished a gallant sixth behind Grundy in 1975, was very much the Wildenstein second string.

Yves Saint-Martin had PAWNEESE out of the stalls in a flash and set out to dictate the pace. Bruni, on the other hand, again lost ground at the start, swerving left and causing Piggott to lose an iron. As PAWNEESE scorched along at the head of the field, followed by Ashmore, Malacate and Youth, Bruni was all of five lengths adrift of the struggling Duke of Marmalade in the rear. At the halfway point, Piggott began to move his mount through the field. At the four furlong marker, however, his progress was temporarily impeded by the weakening Coin of Gold.

Sweeping into the home straight, PAWNEESE, still going easily, led the field. In behind came a closely packed group made up of Ashmore, Malacate, Youth, Orange Bay, Dakota, and Bruni. At this point, the favourite, Youth, lost any chance he may have had by running wide around the bend. Having lost vital ground, he quickly dropped out of contention.

With two furlongs to run, three horses were still in with a chance of catching the leader–Bruni, Orange Bay and the outsider Dakota. As Bruni and Orange Bay came to challenge PAWNEESE down the centre of the course, Dakota, having hung sharply left all the way up the straight, made his run on the stands side. In a memorable finish, the filly, under strong pressure from her pilot, just held the challenge of Bruni by a rapidly diminishing length, with Orange Bay only a short head behind in third place. Dakota, sent off at 80–1, ran the race of his life to finish fourth.

The major disappointment of the race was undoubtedly Youth. He had held a promising position at Swinley Bottom, but unfortunately, Freddie Head's liking for impromptu sightseeing tours of English racecourses brought about a premature end to his challenge. The Italian-trained Duke of Marmalade, who had finished last of the ten runners, failed a post-race dope test.

PAWNEESE was only the fourth filly to win the King George, Aunt Edith, Park Top, and Dahlia having previously been successful.

After Ascot, PAWNEESE lost her form, and ran disappointingly in the Prix Vermeille, and in the Arc, where she finished a remote seventeenth behind Ivanjica. But during the summer of 1976 she was undoubtedly the best middle-distance performer of either sex in Europe. Her victories in the Oaks and the King George, together with those of Flying Water and Crow, enabled Daniel Wildenstein to lead the Owners List in Britain.

Unfortunately for her owner, PAWNEESE made little impact at stud, while Youth, her Ascot victim, went on to sire the 1983 Epsom Derby and 1984 King George winner, Teenoso.

## 1976

### KING GEORGE VI AND QUEEN ELIZABETH DIAMOND STAKES

£81,508    1m 4f

July 24, 1976

| 1 PAWNEESE (FR) | 3 8–5 | Y. Saint-Martin. b.f. by Carvin–Plencia |
|---|---|---|
| 2 BRUNI | 4 9–7 | L. Piggott. gr.c. by Sea Hawk II–Bombazine |
| 3 ORANGE BAY | 4 9–7 | P. Eddery. b.c. by Canisbay–Orange Triumph |
| 4 DAKOTA (b) | 5 9–7 | A. Barclay. br.h. by Stupendous–Ardneasken |
| 5 MALACATE (USA) | 3 8–8 | P. Paquet. b.c. by Lucky Debonair–Eyeshadow |
| 6 COIN OF GOLD | 3 8–8 | W. Carson. ch.c. by Welsh Pageant–Mesopotamia |
| 7 RECORD RUN | 5 9–7 | E. Eldin. b.h. by Track Spare–Bench Game |
| 8 ASHMORE | 5 9–7 | W. Pyers. b.h. by Luthier–Almyre |
| 9 YOUTH (USA) | 3 8–8 | F. Head. b.c. by Ack Ack–Gazala |
| 10 DUKE OF MARMALADE (USA) (b) | 5 9–7 | S. Fancera. b.h. by Vaguely Noble–Mock Orange |

10 Ran

Going – Firm

Distances: 1,sht hd,¾,¾,4

Time: 2:29.36

S.P. 15–8 YOUTH, 9–4 PAWNEESE, 6–1 BRUNI, 13–2 MALACATE, 10–1 ORANGE BAY, 22–1 ASHMORE, 40–1 RECORD RUN, 80–1 DAKOTA, 100–1 OTHERS

Winner trained by A. Penna at Chantilly: owned by D. Wildenstein: bred by Dayton Ltd

Timeform rating of winner 131

# 1977

Gather together a syndicate of well-heeled businessmen, buy a group of extremely well bred yearlings, put them into training with the greatest trainer in the world, win the odd Classic or two and then syndicate your highly desirable new stallion (or stallions if you're lucky) to yield a nice fat profit on the initial investment.

In 1975 Robert Sangster and his partners, Vincent O'Brien, Alan Clore, David Ackroyd and the Honourable Simon Fraser, set out to turn just such a pipe dream into reality. Of course there were risks involved. What if the expensive yearlings proved to be selling-platers? What if the bloodstock industry were hit by another depression? The potential rewards, however, made the calculated gamble worth taking.

The rock on which the whole operation based its foundation was the unique talent of Vincent O'Brien. O'Brien had an almost mystical ability to spot a potential champion in a group of unfurnished yearlings. He was able to visualise the finished product where others saw only the unformed prototype. Thanks to O'Brien's exceptional judgement, the syndicate hit the jackpot with their first batch of yearlings which included the top-class colts Be My Guest, Artaius and the 1977 King George winner, THE MINSTREL.

To his eternal credit, Vincent O'Brien had spotted the potential of the Northern Dancer blood before most Europeans had even heard of the little Canadian stallion. At the 1975 Keeneland Sales, O'Brien's attention was captured by a flashy chestnut with four white socks and a striking white blaze. The colt's pedigree was impeccable. By Northern Dancer out of a half-sister to O'Brien's champion Nijinsky, he was a most imposing individual despite being rather on the small side. The colt, later named THE MINSTREL, was secured for the syndicate with a bid of $200,000.

THE MINSTREL made his racecourse debut in the Moy Stakes at the Curragh. His home reputation had preceded him and he started the 4–9 favourite in a field of twelve. The little horse did not let his supporters down, coming home by five lengths and setting a new course record for good measure. After landing the Larkspur Stakes at Leopardstown, THE MINSTREL maintained his unbeaten record in the Group One Dewhurst Stakes at Newmarket, beating Saros by an easy four lengths. At the close of the 1976 season, THE MINSTREL was rated eight pounds behind Noel Murless's J. O. Tobin in the Free Handicap.

THE MINSTREL was made the 6–5 favourite for the Two Thousand Guineas on the strength of his victory in the Ascot Trial. In a tight finish to the first colts' Classic he was beaten into third place by Nebbiolo and Tachypous. But the little chestnut gained his revenge on Nebbiolo in the Irish Two Thousand Guineas, beating the English Guineas winner by a length, the pair finishing second and third to the Stuart-Murless trained Pampapaul.

There had been doubts about THE MINSTREL's ability to stay one and a half miles, but after the Irish Two Thousand Guineas, Lester Piggott, the colt's regular partner since his second race, advised O'Brien to run the horse at Epsom.

O'Brien was worried about the effects the Derby preliminaries might have on his little horse. Ever the perfectionist, the Tipperary trainer stuffed the horse's ears with cotton wool in order to shut out some of the barrage of sound created by the excitement of Derby day. Once the horse was safely down at the start, assistant trainer John Gosden removed the wool.

Under the most inspirational ride from Piggott, THE MINSTREL courageously got up on the line to beat Hot Grove by a neck in a manner reminiscent of the 1972 finish between Roberto and Rheingold. Piggott's confidence in the horse had been fully justified; the syndicate had an Epsom Derby winner on their hands.

Despite swerving violently across the course in the closing stages, THE MINSTREL survived an objection by the runner-up Lucky Sovereign, to add the Irish Sweeps Derby to his list of Group race victories. THE MINSTREL's next race, his sixth in sixteen weeks, would be against his elders in the King George at Ascot.

From a record entry of 184, eleven runners went to the post for the 1977 King George. THE MINSTREL faced opposition of the highest calibre.

Spearheading the French challenge were the four-year-olds Crow and Exceller and the year younger Crystal Palace. Angel Penna, successful with Pawneese in 1976, was seeking a King George double with the 1976 St Leger winner Crow. Exceller carried the light and dark green checked Bunker Hunt colours successfully carried by Dahlia in 1973 and 1974. With victories in the Coronation Cup and the Grand Prix de Saint-Cloud to his credit, Exceller would be a tough nut to crack. François Mathet, trainer of Exceller, also saddled the Prix du Jockey Club winner Crystal Palace who ran in the colours of Baron Guy de Rothschild.

The 1977 line-up was truly international, with Trainers Seat travelling from Norway, Mart Lane and THE MINSTREL representing Ireland, and Rheffissimo, a French-bred colt trained at Newmarket by an Italian, carrying the colours of his Spanish owner, the Count of Villapadierna.

Of the home-trained contenders, the five-year-olds Bruni and Orange Bay looked the most dangerous. Bruni, the 1975 St Leger winner, had finished runner-up to the flying filly Pawneese in the last King George. In his two runs prior to Ascot, the grey had passed the post first in the Henry II Stakes at Sandown only to be disqualified for bumping the runner-up Grey Baron, and then finished a well-beaten fourth behind Sagaro in the Ascot Gold Cup. Orange Bay had also run with merit in the previous King George, coming home in third place, a short head behind Bruni. In the current season however, Peter Walwyn's charge had failed to distinguish himself. After a lacklustre display in the John Porter Stakes, he struggled to win a poor contest for the Aston Park Stakes at Newbury. On his only other run Orange Bay had finished last of seven in the Hardwicke Stakes behind the O'Brien-trained Meneval. Walwyn was hopeful, however, that the fitting of blinkers would herald a return to form at Ascot.

Brilliant sunshine brought racegoers in their thousands to witness the twenty-seventh running of the King George. But the hot sticky conditions caused several of the runners to become lathered in sweat with THE MINSTREL and Orange Bay two of the worst sufferers.

First to show from the stalls was Mart Lane, tracked by the Joe

Mercer-ridden Lucky Wednesday. Piggott, having missed the break, had THE MINSTREL at the rear of the field. At the halfway point, Mart Lane still held the lead followed closely by Rheffissimo, Lucky Wednesday and Trainers Seat. In behind tightly bunched came Bruni, Crystal Palace, Exceller and Norfolk Air. After this group and going easily, THE MINSTREL matched strides with Orange Bay, with Crow the back marker.

Five furlongs out, Piggott and Eddery made their moves simultaneously. Initially, Orange Bay found the better turn of foot and moved smoothly into third place on the home turn. THE MINSTREL still had five horses in front of him turning for home. With three furlongs to run, there were four horses still in with a chance, Orange Bay, Exceller, THE MINSTREL and Crystal Palace. But in a matter of strides the French challenge had petered out, leaving Orange Bay and THE MINSTREL to fight out the finish.

At the furlong pole Eddery had a slight lead, but Piggott dug deep into THE MINSTREL's reserves and began to urge his mount ahead, hitting the front with two hundred yards to run. The blinkered Orange Bay fought like a tiger all the way to the line, but the THE MINSTREL, with the rails to help him, just had the edge, holding on in the dying strides to win a memorable race by the shortest of short heads. The third horse, Exceller, was a further length and a half behind, followed home by his compatriot Crystal Palace. The third French raider, Crow, was a major disappointment, finishing tenth of the eleven runners after trailing the field for most of the race.

Vincent O'Brien had landed his third King George, while Piggott had won the race for an amazing sixth time.

After the race, the syndicate sold a half share in THE MINSTREL back to his breeder E. P. Taylor for a reputed $4.1 million. The dream had become reality.

Due to an outbreak of contagious metritis, which was threatening the export of bloodstock from Britain, it was decided to send THE MINSTREL to the USA as quickly as possible, and so the little chestnut began his stallion duties at Windfields Farm in Maryland. He was later moved to Overbrook Farm in Kentucky.

THE MINSTREL has stamped his stock with the same combination of toughness and ability which he himself displayed during his racing career. Now a highly successful stallion, THE MINSTREL's most notable progeny include the 1983 Poule d'Essai des Poulains winner L'Emigrant, the 1988 Irish Oaks dead heater Melodist, and the 1989 One Thousand Guineas heroine Musical Bliss.

## 1977

### KING GEORGE VI AND QUEEN ELIZABETH DIAMOND STAKES (GROUP ONE)

£88,355    1m 4f

July 23, 1977

| | | | |
|---|---|---|---|
| 1 | THE MINSTREL (CAN) | 3 8–8 | L. Piggott. ch.c. by Northern Dancer–Fleur |
| 2 | ORANGE BAY (b) | 5 9–7 | P. Eddery. b.h. by Canisbay–Orange Triumph |
| 3 | EXCELLER (USA) | 4 9–7 | F. Head. b.c. by Vaguely Noble–Too Bold |
| 4 | CRYSTAL PALACE (FR) | 3 8–8 | G. Dubrœucq. gr.c. by Caro–Hermieres |
| 5 | NORFOLK AIR (b) | 4 9–7 | G. Starkey. br.c. by Blakeney–Melody Maid |
| 6 | LUCKY WEDNESDAY | 4 9–7 | J. Mercer. br.c. by Roi Soleil–Pavlova |
| 7 | BRUNI | 5 9–7 | B. Taylor. gr.h. by Sea Hawk II–Bombazine |
| 8 | MART LANE | 4 9–7 | E. Hide. br.c. by Le Lavanstell–Marians |
| 9 | TRAINERS SEAT | 4 9–7 | D. Lacy. b.c. by Tamerlane–Bottoms Up |
| 10 | CROW (FR) | 4 9–7 | Y. Saint-Martin. ch.c. by Exbury–Carmosina |
| 11 | RHEFFISSIMO (FR) | 4 9–7 | B. Raymond. ch.c. by Rheffic–La Sanctissima |

11 Ran

Going – Good

Distances: sht hd,1½,3,1½,¾

Time: 2:30.48

S.P. 7–4 THE MINSTREL, 100–30 CROW, 11–2 EXCELLER, 6–1 CRYSTAL PALACE, 11–1 BRUNI, 16–1 LUCKY WEDNESDAY, 20–1 ORANGE BAY, 25–1 MART LANE, 50–1 RHEFFISSIMO, 66–1 OTHERS

Winner trained by M. V. O'Brien at Cashel, Co Tipperary: owned by Mr R. Sangster: bred by Mr E. P. Taylor in Canada

Timeform rating of winner 135

# 1978

How frustrating it is to see stallions sold to stand abroad produce top-class performers immediately they leave these shores. A prime example of this all too familiar trend is ILE DE BOURBON. Having proved rather disappointing as a sire, the son of Nijinsky was exported to Japan in 1987. Sure enough, a top-class ILE DE BOURBON colt emerged in the shape of Kahyasi, the 1988 Epsom Derby winner – a perfect manifestation of Sod's Law.

ILE DE BOURBON, the 1978 King George winner, had been a maiden until four weeks before Ascot. A rather lightly built, slow-maturing type, he had been given plenty of time to realise his potential.

The colt was bred by Mrs Jane Engelhard whose late husband, Charles, had owned both the sire Nijinsky and the dam, Roseliere, winner of the 1968 Prix de Diane. This made ILE DE BOURBON a half-brother to the outstanding filly Rose Bowl, also trained at Blewbury by Fulke Johnson Houghton who owned him in partnership with his mother, Helen, bloodstock agent David McCall and Sir Philip Oppenheimer, Chairman of De Beers, the King George sponsors.

ILE DE BOURBON was asked to race only twice as a two-year-old. After finishing fourth at Ascot in September, he ran ninth of twelve behind Dactylographer in the William Hill Futurity at Doncaster. But the colt made outstanding progress during the winter, giving rise to great expectations at Blewbury.

On his seasonal reappearance, ILE DE BOURBON ran the future Derby winner Shirley Heights to a short head in a blood and thunder finish for the Heathorn Stakes at Newmarket. Many observers felt that Piggott had been too hard on his inexperienced mount and expected the horse's future performances to suffer in consequence. Piggott was again in the saddle when ILE DE BOURBON contested the

Predominate Stakes at Goodwood. Under another punishing ride, the colt was beaten by a length and a half by the Ian Balding-trained English Harbour.

Fortune plays a major part in the affairs of the Turf. ILE DE BOURBON's next outing was to be in the King Edward VII Stakes at Royal Ascot. Piggott chose to abandon Johnson Houghton's colt in favour of the Vincent O'Brien-trained Stradavinsky. In consequence, John Reid, only one season out of his apprenticeship, came in for the ride on ILE DE BOURBON.

Although retained by Johnson Houghton, the young Ulsterman had seen most of the stable's better horses ridden to victory by "the Long Fellow". Reid was determined to grasp the nettle of opportunity with both hands. In a finish full of dramatic irony, ILE DE BOURBON lost his maiden status at the expense of Stradavinsky, who failed to cope with his opponent's late challenge, going under by two and a half lengths.

Johnson Houghton knew his horse was capable of further improvement and so courageously decided to take on the established stars in the King George.

1978 saw the largest King George field for twenty-four years. The fourteen runners included representatives from America, New Zealand, France and Ireland. The French challenge was particularly strong. Leading the French attack was the handsome bay Acamas. In landing the 1978 Prix du Jockey Club, Acamas had provided Mill Reef with his first Derby winner. With the Epsom and Irish Derby winner, Shirley Heights, bypassing the King George in favour of the St Leger, Acamas was sent off the 2–1 favourite at Ascot. The French also expected bold performances from Guadanini, winner of the Grand Prix de Saint-Cloud; Trillion, successful in the Prix Ganay, and from the Hardwicke Stakes winner, Moncontour.

The relative prospects of the two New Zealand-bred runners, Balmerino and Silver Lad, were highlighted by their starting prices, Balmerino finding support at 10–1, while Silver Lad was friendless in the market at 50–1. Balmerino, runner-up to Alleged in the 1977 Arc, had run a series of respectable races in 1978. After beating Uncle Pokey in the Clive Graham Stakes at Goodwood, he had finished second behind Crow in the Coronation Cup, third to Moncontour in the Hardwicke Stakes and second to Gunner B in the

Coral Eclipse. However, on more than one occasion he had appeared somewhat less than enthusiastic about the business in hand and was certainly not the type of horse on which to plunge heavily.

From Ireland came the four-year-old Orchestra, winner of the John Porter Stakes and the three-year-old Exdirectory. The Paddy Prendergast-trained Exdirectory had run a splendid race on his previous appearance, losing out by a head to Shirley Heights in the Irish Sweeps Derby.

Apart from the relatively inexperienced ILE DE BOURBON, the main hope of keeping the prize at home rested with the Queen's Royal Palace filly Dunfermline and with the Barry Hills-trained three-year-old Hawaiian Sound.

Dunfermline, heroine of the 1977 Oaks and St Leger, had just one run prior to the King George. It must be said that in finishing second to Moncontour in the Hardwicke Stakes, she disappointed her connections who were far from certain that she had trained on from three to four. Major Hern decided to give his filly the chance to show her true form in the King George where she would have the benefit of a pacemaker, Sea Boat.

Hawaiian Sound, on the other hand, had been a model of consistency in 1978. After comfortably winning his first two races, the son of Hawaii was beaten by a neck in the Chester Vase, a head in the Epsom Derby and a head and a neck in the Irish Sweeps Derby. The legendary American Bill Shoemaker, who partnered the horse at Epsom and the Curragh, retained the ride at Ascot.

The American challenger That's a Nice, and the French-trained Rex Magna were not rated serious contenders.

Sea Boat did his job extremely well, bouncing out of the gate and dictating the pace for nine furlongs. Hawaiian Sound, normally a front-runner, had to be content with a position in behind Sea Boat and Dunfermline.

At the mile post, the fourteen runners were stretched out in Indian file. Turning for home, Sea Boat still had the lead from the hard-ridden Dunfermline with ILE DE BOURBON, still on the bridle, cruising in behind. After these came Hawaiian Sound, Balmerino, Moncontour and Acamas, with the rest of the field already beaten.

Having made the turn, Dunfermline took the lead from her pacemaker, but the Queen's filly had been under pressure from fully four furlongs out, and in a matter of strides ILE DE BOURBON had flashed past her as if she were standing still. Bouncing off the firm ground, ILE DE BOURBON, still on the bit, kicked for home. At this point only Acamas and Hawaiian Sound were in with a chance of catching the leader.

At the furlong pole, Acamas, his rounded action unsuited to the top-of-the-ground conditions, began to hang to his left away from Saint-Martin's whip. As ILE DE BOURBON crossed the line in the hands of a jubilant John Reid, Shoemaker and Saint-Martin fought for second place, the Frenchman just getting the decision by a neck.

At a subsequent inquiry, Acamas was disqualified after the prohibited substance salicylic acid was found in the horse's post-race urine sample.

Strictly on form, ILE DE BOURBON emerged from his King George victory a superior horse to the dual Derby winner Shirley Heights.

After Ascot, ILE DE BOURBON went on to win the Geoffrey Freer Stakes at Newbury and to become the first King George winner to contest the St Leger since his sire Nijinsky in 1970. Unfortunately, the mile and six furlongs of the St Leger proved too much for ILE DE BOURBON, the colt finishing sixth to the Clive Brittain-trained Julio Mariner.

His sporting connections decided to keep ILE DE BOURBON in training as a four-year-old, hoping he would continue to improve as he developed physically. The decision seemed to be vindicated when the colt won his first two races of 1979, the Clive Graham Stakes and the Coronation Cup.

Unhappily, ILE DE BOURBON contracted a virus after Epsom which prevented him from attempting a King George double. On his return to the racecourse he was merely a shadow of his former self and he was comprehensively beaten by Cracaval in the September Stakes at Kempton. After running a disappointing fourteenth behind Three Troikas in the Arc, connections announced that ILE DE BOURBON had run his last race.

The son of Nijinsky was retired to Banstead Stud in Newmarket. His pedigree and his racecourse achievements made ILE DE BOURBON an outstanding stallion prospect. We lacked the patience, however, to see his potential realised and our loss is Japan's gain.

## 1978

## KING GEORGE VI AND QUEEN ELIZABETH DIAMOND STAKES (GROUP ONE)

£98,120      1m 4f

July 22, 1978

| | | | |
|---|---|---|---|
| 1 ILE DE BOURBON (USA) | 3 8–8 | J. Reid. br.c. by Nijinsky–Roseliere | |
| 2 ACAMAS (FR) | 3 8–8 | Y. Saint-Martin. b.c. by Mill Reef–Licata | |
| 3 HAWAIIAN SOUND (USA) | 3 8–8 | W. Shoemaker. b.c. by Hawaii–Sound Of Success | |
| 4 MONTCONTOUR (FR) | 4 9–7 | A. Lequeux. br.c. by Luthier II–Moskvitcha | |
| 5 BALMERINO (NZ) | 6 9–7 | M. Campbell. b.h. by Trictrac–Dulcie | |
| 6 EXDIRECTORY | 3 8–8 | P. Eddery. ch.c. by Ballymore–Regal Bell | |
| 7 GUADININI (FR) | 4 9–7 | M. Philipperon. ch.c. by Luthier II–Ilrem | |
| 8 DUNFERMLINE | 4 9–4 | W. Carson. b.f. by Royal Palace–Strathcona | |
| 9 ORCHESTRA | 4 9–7 | R. Carroll. ch.c. by Tudor Music–Golden Moss | |
| 10 SILVER LAD (NZ) | 5 9–7 | H. White. b.h. by Silver Dream–Leta Filou | |
| 11 REX MAGNA (FR) | 4 9–7 | P. Paquet. br.c. by Right Royal V–Chambre d'Amour | |
| 12 TRILLION (USA) | 4 9–4 | L. Piggott. b.f. by Hail to Reason–Margarethen | |
| 13 SEA BOAT (b) | 4 9–7 | A. Bond. b.c. by Royal Palace–Anchor | |
| 14 THAT'S A NICE (USA) | 4 9–7 | G. Starkey. ch.c. by Hey Good Lookin–Our Bonnie S | |

14 Ran

Going – Firm

Distances: 1½,nk,1½,2,¾,1½

Time: 2:30.53

S.P. 2—1 ACAMAS, 9—2 DUNFERMLINE, 7—1 TRILLION, 9—1 EXDIRECTORY, HAWAIIAN SOUND, 10—1 BALMERINO, GUADANINI, 12—1 ILE DE BOURBON, 25—1 MONCONTOUR, 33—1 REX MAGNA, THAT'S A NICE, 50—1 SILVER LAD, 66—1 ORCHESTRA, 200—1 SEA BOAT

Winner trained by Fulke Johnson Houghton at Blewbury: owned by Mr A. McCall: bred by Mrs C. Engelhard in USA

Timeform rating of winner 133

# 1979

"He was bloody horrible to ride, very lethargic." Hardly the predictable comment to make about a champion, but that is how Willie Carson described the 1979 Racehorse of the Year, TROY. Being possessed of an ultraphlegmatic temperament, TROY did nothing in a hurry; he needed time to warm up in his races. Once he had stoked up the engine, however, the son of Petingo was an awesome sight.

By a strange quirk of fate, both of TROY's parents died the year he was foaled. His sire, Petingo, was a high-class performer, winning the Gimcrack, and finishing runner-up to Sir Ivor in the Two Thousand Guineas, while his dam, La Milo, had produced six consecutive winners prior to TROY.

Owned in partnership by Sir Michael Sobell, and his son-in-law, Sir Arnold Weinstock, TROY gave plenty of notice of his Classic potential during his first season in training. After filling the runner-up spot on his debut in a Salisbury maiden, he won the Plantation Stakes at Newmarket and the Lanson Champagne Stakes at Goodwood. In the latter race, he gave Ela-Mana-Mou three pounds and a two-and-a-half-length beating. Guy Harwood's colt gained his revenge in the Royal Lodge Stakes at Ascot, just getting up in the closing stages to beat TROY by three-quarters of a length. With two wins and two seconds from four starts, TROY was rated only seven pounds behind the leading two-year-old of 1978, the Bruce Hobbs-trained Tromos.

It had been seven years since Major Hern had had a truly great colt in his care. While nobody at West Ilsley believed TROY would match the Brigadier's record-breaking achievements, there was an unmistakable air of expectation around the yard throughout the winter months.

TROY's path to Classic glory took him to Sandown and Goodwood in the spring of 1979. After landing the Sandown Classic Trial and the Predominate Stakes, he lined up for the 200th Derby, the 6–1 second favourite. Two furlongs from home his supporters must have given up all hope as Carson could be seen pumping away back in eighth place. Suddenly, however, the engine started to motor, and TROY flew past his rivals as if they were wearing hob-nailed boots. His seven-length victory was the widest winning margin since Manna won the Derby by the same distance back in 1925.

The Derby form was made to look even better when TROY went on to an easy four-length success in the Irish Sweeps Derby at the Curragh and Dickens Hill, runner-up in both Classics, beat the older horses in the Coral-Eclipse.

Not surprisingly Dickens Hill side-stepped another clash with TROY in the King George. Indeed, Major Hern's dual Classic winner scared off most of Europe's best middle-distance horses. Despite meeting his elders for the first time in his career, TROY was sent off the 2–5 favourite at Ascot. With just seven horses facing the starter, the 1979 race saw the smallest field since 1970.

With Road to Glory acting as a pacemaker for TROY and Ryan Price's M-Lolshan running out of his class, the odds-on favourite had only four serious rivals to contend with.

Ela-Mana-Mou, the only other three-year-old in the race, had finished over ten lengths behind TROY at Epsom, and appeared to have an impossible task at level weights. The French challenger Gay Mecene also had the beating of Ela-Mana-Mou, having beaten Guy Harwood's colt by four lengths when winning the Grand Prix de Saint-Cloud. He was, however, a temperamental character whose form fluctuated with his moods. The much travelled Telescopico was an unknown quantity. Equating Argentinian form with European form is virtually impossible, yet Chantilly-based trainer Maurice Zilber paid $1.2 million for the colt at the end of the 1978 season. The King George would reveal whether the enigmatic trainer had acquired a bargain or been sold a dud.

Swiss Maid, the only filly in the field, was a Jekyll and Hyde character, who on a good day was more than capable of beating the best horses in Europe. On a bad day, she could quite easily lose her race before the stalls had even opened by letting her temperament get the better of her. In the 1978 Champion Stakes she was on her best behaviour, coasting home from a top-class field, but in the 1979 Coral Eclipse, the demons had possessed her with such ferocity that she worked herself into a frenzy and finished stone last. Those intrepid punters who supported her for the King George would not know their fate until she was safely in the stalls. In the event, Swiss Maid put up only minimal resistance and consented to enter the stalls at the second attempt.

As the stalls burst open, the blinkered Road to Glory was rushed into the lead as expected. The pace was, however, not as punishing as the Hern camp had hoped for, and TROY could be seen fighting for his head in fifth place. After a mile, Road to Glory still held the lead, two lengths ahead of Telescopico, Ela-Mana-Mou, and TROY who were all closely bunched. After this group came M-Lolshan, Gay Mecene and the filly Swiss Maid.

Turning for home, the race began to develop in earnest as the pacemaker began to weaken. The fact that Road to Glory had held the advantage for so long was an indication of how moderate a pace he had set. As the field made the right-handed sweep into the straight, TROY skidded on the baked ground, losing his hind legs for a stride or two. Swiss Maid, travelling in the favourite's slipstream, appeared to slip on the same patch of ground, losing all momentum and two valuable lengths. For her the race was as good as over.

TROY, however, recovered well and began to eat up the ground in the home straight. As Carson pulled the favourite to the outside of the field to deliver his challenge, the noise from the packed stands reached deafening proportions. With two furlongs to run Ela-Mana-Mou hit the front under strong driving from Greville Starkey. Unfortunately for the Harwood camp, danger in the blue and yellow Sobell colours was hovering alongside.

TROY drew level with Ela-Mana-Mou just below the distance, and after matching strides for what seemed like an eternity, eased ahead of his rival inside the final furlong. As Ela-Mana-Mou ran out of steam, Gay Mecene could be seen making relentless progress on the wide outside. Two back-handers from Carson were all that was necessary to repel the Gallic challenge, TROY crossing the finishing line a length and a half to the good. Ela-Mana-Mou held third place by three parts of a length.

TROY's performance at Ascot was workmanlike rather than spectacular, but to be fair he was probably unhappy on the bone hard ground.

The Benson and Hedges Gold Cup at York was TROY's next engagement. Over the years the ten-furlong race had been a graveyard for favourites, Brigadier Gerard and Grundy being just two of the mighty to have fallen. TROY duly won, but he had to work hard to beat Paul Cole's Crimson Beau.

Connections were hopeful that TROY would conclude his racing career in a blaze of glory by landing the Prix de l'Arc de Triomphe at Longchamp. Unfortunately the fairy-tale ending failed to materialise and TROY finished third behind the French-trained pair Three Troikas and Le Marmot.

TROY retired to the Highclere Stud in Newbury with record earnings of £415,735. He made a most encouraging start to his stallion career before prematurely dying from a perforated intestine in 1983.

The 1970s were vintage years in the history of the Turf, providing us with champions like Nijinsky, Mill Reef, Brigadier Gerard and Grundy. To this roll of honour we must add the name of the outstanding racehorse of 1979, TROY.

# 1979

## KING GEORGE VI AND QUEEN ELIZABETH DIAMOND STAKES (GROUP ONE)

£94,460    1m 4f

July 28, 1979

| | | | |
|---|---|---|---|
| 1 TROY | 3 8–8 | W. Carson. b.c. by Petingo–La Milo | |
| 2 GAY MECENE (FR) | 4 9–7 | F. Head. b.c. by Vaguely Noble–Gay Misile | |
| 3 ELA-MANA-MOU | 3 8–8 | G. Starkey. b.c. by Pitcairn–Rose Bertin | |
| 4 M-LOLSHAN | 4 9–7 | B. Taylor. br.c. by Levmoss–Supreme Lady | |
| 5 TELESCOPICO (ARG) | 4 9–7 | A. Lequeux. b.c. by Table Play–Filipina | |
| 6 ROAD TO GLORY (FR) (b) | 4 9–7 | B. Procter. b.c. by Sir Gaylord–Boulevard | |
| 7 SWISS MAID | 4 9–4 | P. Eddery. b.f. by Welsh Pageant–Hornton Grange | |

7 Ran

Going – Firm

Distances: 1½,3,¾,¾,3,4

Time: 2:33.75

S.P. 2–5 TROY, 15–2 ELA-MANA-MOU, 17–2 GAY MECENE, 10–1 SWISS MAID, 20–1 TELESCOPICO, 25–1 M-LOLSHAN, 300–1 ROAD TO GLORY

Winner trained by Major Hern at West Ilsley: owned by Sir Michael Sobell: bred by Ballymacoll Stud

Timeform rating of winner 137

# 1980

For the second successive year the King George went to an inmate of Major Hern's West Ilsley Stables, ELA-MANA-MOU following in the hoofprints of the 1979 winner Troy.

Until the King George, ELA-MANA-MOU had to a certain extent lived in the shadow of his stable companion, Henbit. The injury Henbit sustained in the closing stages of his Derby victory cleared the way for ELA-MANA-MOU's assault on the Ascot showpiece. Although the Hern camp were disappointed that their Blue Riband winner would not be in the King George field, they were extremely fortunate to have a first-rate substitute in ELA-MANA-MOU.

Purchased for only 4,500 guineas as a yearling by Mrs Audrey Muinos, the Pitcairn colt was trained by Guy Harwood as a two- and three-year-old. At two ELA-MANA-MOU won four of his five races, culminating, ironically, in a three-quarter-length victory over Major Hern's TROY in the Royal Lodge Stakes.

In his second season, ELA-MANA-MOU started favourite for the Derby, but failed to match Troy's brilliant turn of foot, eventually finishing a respectable fourth. After making all to land the King Edward VII Stakes at Royal Ascot, he travelled to France for the Grand Prix de Saint-Cloud. Without ever looking likely to beat Gay Mecene, he collected second prize, going under by four lengths.

ELA-MANA-MOU then ran a courageous race in the 1979 King George, where, despite pulling a muscle, he took third place behind Troy and Gay Mecene.

Despite a twelve-week rest, the Pitcairn colt still looked out of sorts in his final race of 1979 when after finishing a poor sixth behind Northern Baby in the Champion Stakes, he was found to be running a temperature.

In December 1979, Audrey Muinos sold ELA-MANA-MOU for a

reported £500,000 to a partnership consisting of Tim Rogers and various members of the Weinstock family. The horse was to race in the pale blue and yellow colours of Simon Weinstock and be trained by Major Hern. The partnership made a sound investment. At three, ELA-MANA-MOU had been just short of top-class, but the colt improved to such an extent during his fourth year that he was valued at £3.2 million at the end of the 1980 season.

After landing the Group Three Earl of Sefton Stakes for his new connections, ELA-MANA-MOU moved up the Pattern Race scale with wins in the Group Two Prince of Wales Stakes and the Group One Coral Eclipse Stakes. In the latter race he accounted for the highly regarded Henry Cecil runner Hello Gorgeous by three-quarters of a length. With stablemate Henbit injured, Major Hern then declared ELA-MANA-MOU for the King George where he faced nine opponents.

The 1980 King George field was somewhat sub-standard in comparison with previous contests. Although there were three Classic winners in the line-up, there was no obvious middle-distance champion on parade.

Despite suffering a minor injury on the journey from France, François Boutin's four-year-old colt Le Marmot led the market at 7–4. Runner-up in both the 1979 Prix du Jockey Club and the 1979 Arc, Le Marmot had earned his position as favourite with a length and a half victory over the Arc-winning filly Three Troikas in the Prix Ganay at Longchamp in May. On paper he appeared the chief danger to ELA-MANA-MOU, the pair dominating the market almost to the exclusion of the rest of the field.

The other French-trained runner, Dunette, was one of the best fillies in her native country in 1979, with a success in the Prix de Diane de Revlon to her credit. She had continued her winning ways in the 1980 Grand Prix de Saint-Cloud, where she dead heated for first place with Shakapour.

Ian Balding's filly Mrs Penny had won the latest running of the Prix de Diane de Revlon, beating Aryenne in a tight finish. The top two-year-old filly of 1979 had the benefit of Lester Piggott's services at Ascot, the "maestro" having chosen Mrs Penny in preference to Vincent O'Brien's colt Gregorian. A brown colt by Graustark, Gregorian had won both the Westbury Stakes and the Brigadier Gerard Stakes prior to finishing a well-beaten third behind ELA-MANA-MOU in the Eclipse.

[ 132 ]

The third Classic winner in the field was the Bruce Hobbs-trained Tyrnavos. Successful in a sub-standard Irish Sweeps Derby, Tyrnavos was out of that remarkable winner-producing mare Stilvi.

Of the remainder of the field, only Main Reef could be given a chance. The half-brother to Moonlight Night was not an easy ride, often cocking his head to one side when under pressure. He would need to return to the form which saw him land the St Simon Stakes in 1979 if he were to pose a serious threat.

In the event, the 1980 King George was to produce one of the most exciting finishes in the history of the race.

Eddie Hide kicked Tyrnavos into an early lead closely tracked by Majestic Maharaj and the Hern second string, More Light. After a mile Tyrnavos still held the lead, but several horses were still going well. The chestnut filly Mrs Penny was cruising in fourth place, just ahead of ELA-MANA-MOU.

At the four furlong pole, Carson made his move, rushing his mount past the weakening Tyrnavos and into a length lead. Carson's manoeuvre caught many of his rivals flat-footed. In a matter of strides, More Light, Pelerin, Main Reef and Majestic Maharaj were under pressure and out of the race. With two furlongs to run, the favourite Le Marmot had also given up the ghost, leaving just four horses in with a chance of the prize.

At the head of the field, Carson was riding ELA-MANA-MOU for all he was worth. Piggott, on the other hand, had hardly moved a muscle on Mrs Penny who was still on the bridle. As the two principals drew away from the tail-swishing Gregorian, the Ascot crowd rose as one to cheer home the gallant protagonists.

With Piggott finally forced to go for his stick, the issue remained in doubt until the very last strides. ELA-MANA-MOU fought off his younger rival gamely, responding courageously to every stroke of his rider's whip. The filly had no more to give. At the post ELA-MANA-MOU had three-quarters of a length to spare. Gregorian finished third, five lengths behind Mrs Penny.

ELA-MANA-MOU made his final racecourse appearance in the Arc where, after leading until inside the final furlong, he finished third, beaten half a length and a short head by Detroit and Argument.

The winner of ten of his sixteen races, and only once out of the frame, ELA-MANA-MOU retired to stand at the Simmonstown Stud in

Ireland. His best produce to date are the 1985 Grand Prix de Paris winner Sumyar, and the 1988 Jockey Club and Hardwicke Stakes winner Almaarad.

# 1980

## KING GEORGE VI AND QUEEN ELIZABETH DIAMOND STAKES (GROUP ONE)

£124,696     1m 4f

July 26, 1980

| 1 | ELA-MANA-MOU | 4 9–7 | W. Carson. b.c. by Pitcairn–Rose Bertin |
|---|---|---|---|
| 2 | MRS PENNY (USA) | 3 8–5 | L. Piggott. ch.f. by Great Nephew–Tananarive |
| 3 | GREGORIAN (USA) | 4 9–7 | T. Murphy. br.c. by Graustark–Natashka |
| 4 | DUNETTE (FR) | 4 9–4 | G. Doleuze. b.f. by Hard To Beat–Pram |
| 5 | LE MARMOT (FR) | 4 9–7 | P. Paquet. b.c. by Amarko–Molinka |
| 6 | MAJESTIC MAHARAJ | 5 9–7 | E. Johnson. br.h. by Taj Dewan–Canaan |
| 7 | MAIN REEF | 4 9–7 | J. Mercer. ch.c. by Mill Reef–Lovely Light |
| 8 | TYRNAVOS | 3 8–8 | E. Hide. b.c. by Blakeney–Stilvi |
| 9 | PELERIN (FR) (b) | 3 8–8 | J. Reid. b.c. by Sir Gaylord–Padrona |
| 10 | MORE LIGHT (b) | 4 9–7 | P. Cook. b.c. by Morston–Death Ray |

10 Ran

Going – Good

Distances: ¾,5,½,¾,7,nk

Time: 2:36.39

S.P. 7–4 LE MARMOT, 11–4 ELA-MANA-MOU, 7–1 TYRNAVOS, 9–1 MRS PENNY, 12–1 DUNETTE, 14–1 MAIN REEF, 25–1 GREGORIAN, PELERIN, 33–1 MORE LIGHT, 100–1 MAJESTIC MAHARAJ

Winner trained by Major Hern at West Ilsley: owned by Mr S. Weinstock: bred by Mr P. Clarke

Timeform rating of winner 132

# 1981

At the start of the 1981 Flat season, the Aga Khan had 147 horses in training. From this collection of equine aristocrats a champion emerged who set the racing world alight.

Initially SHERGAR remained inconspicuous amongst Michael Stoute's multi-million-dollar string of over a hundred horses, and the deep-girthed bay colt by Great Nephew out of Sharmeen, did little serious work until the autumn of his second year.

For his racecourse debut Stoute sent SHERGAR to Newbury for the one-mile Kris Plate. In the hands of Lester Piggott the colt toyed with his rivals before forging clear to win in record time. SHERGAR contested just one other race in 1980, the William Hill Futurity at Doncaster. After looking the likely winner two furlongs out, he just failed to cope with Beldale Flutter who beat him by two and a half lengths. In the European Free Handicap SHERGAR was rated joint thirty-first and was considered a 33–1 Derby outsider throughout the winter.

If SHERGAR had been relatively anonymous as a two-year-old, he soon became the talk of Newmarket with a series of high-class gallops during the spring of 1981. On breeding he was unlikely to have the speed necessary to win a Two Thousand Guineas, and therefore Stoute set about laying the colt out for the Derby.

A spectacular ten-length victory in the Guardian Newspaper Classic Trial over Sandown's mile and a quarter on his seasonal reappearance brought SHERGAR into the public eye, a position he maintained to the end of his life.

The colt went on to underline his Derby prospects with a runaway success in the Chester Vase, where he destroyed Sunley Builds by twelve lengths. Having treated the sharp Chester turns with contempt, connections were confident SHERGAR would be more than capable of handling the idiosyncrasies of Epsom.

At 10–11 on, SHERGAR started the shortest priced Derby favourite since Sir Ivor in 1968. Nineteen-year-old Walter Swinburn, newly appointed as Stoute's stable jockey, was the man in the hot seat, truly a baptism of fire. In one of the most one-sided Classics of modern times, SHERGAR slaughtered his opponents, storming home twelve lengths clear of the useful Glint of Gold, the widest margin of victory ever officially recorded in the Derby.

With Swinburn suspended after falling foul of the Stewards, Piggott was reunited with SHERGAR in the Irish Sweeps Derby. Ridden with an air of outrageous nonchalance, SHERGAR toyed with his eleven opponents before striding away for a four-length victory over Major Hern's Cut Above. Having proved himself the best three-year-old in Britain, SHERGAR was declared for the King George where he would get the chance to compete against older horses.

For the first time in the history of the King George there were no foreign contestants, SHERGAR having frightened off all bar six English-trained challengers.

On all known form his most dangerous opponent was the Henry Candy-trained Master Willie. An extremely consistent chestnut son of High Line, Master Willie had run with credit in the highest class over two seasons. As a three-year-old he had won the Benson and Hedges Gold Cup in addition to filling the runner's-up position in both the Derby and the Champion Stakes. In 1981 he had picked up two Group One victories prior to Ascot, in the Coronation Cup and in the Eclipse Stakes.

Third favourite was the Harry Wragg-trained four-year-old Pelerin. The Sir Gaylord colt had run disappointingly in the 1980 King George but had recaptured his form with a vengeance in 1981, landing both the John Porter Stakes and the Hardwicke Stakes.

St Leger winner Light Cavalry, beaten by three lengths by Pelerin in the Hardwicke Stakes, had only one success to his credit in 1981 – a neck victory over Castle Keep in the Princess of Wales Stakes. Even with Piggott in the saddle he appeared to have only an outsider's chance in the King George.

The 1980 Cumberland Lodge winner Fingal's Cave had missed the first half of the 1981 season with a damaged hock. He had finished a creditable fourth to Master Willie in the Eclipse on his reappearance. By a Gold Cup winner, Ragstone, Fingal's Cave needed every inch of twelve furlongs to show his best form.

Paul Kelleway's filly Madam Gay had scored only one success prior to Ascot. Until she landed the Prix de Diane, the daughter of Star Appeal had always managed to find one too good for her. Nevertheless she had run a series of gutsy races in defeat, most notably her second to Blue Wind in the Oaks.

Cracaval, the outsider of the field at 80–1, had beaten Ile de Bourbon in the 1979 September Stakes, but had shown little form for some time.

Reunited with Walter Swinburn, SHERGAR looked magnificent going to the post and he completely outshone his rivals. His unusual scurrying action would not be inconvenienced by the ground conditions which were officially described as "Good to Firm" and the Stoute camp was brimming over with confidence, having landed the preceding Princess Margaret Stakes with the two-year-old filly, Circus Ring.

Piggott bounced Light Cavalry out of the stalls and into an early lead. With Jim Joel's horse setting only a moderate gallop, Swinburn had a problem settling his mount in the early stages of the race, SHERGAR persistently fighting for his head. Fortunately the pace increased after four furlongs and he consented to settle in behind Light Cavalry and the second horse Master Willie, who moved smoothly into the lead half a mile from home.

Rounding the final turn, Swinburn found himself boxed in on the rails behind Master Willie, Light Cavalry, Fingal's Cave and the improving Madam Gay. With no clear path the Aga Khan's horse looked in serious trouble, but then, as if by magic, a gap appeared between Light Cavalry and the rails. Swinburn pounced on the opening, SHERGAR sprinting through without the slightest hesitation.

The race was decided in an instant as SHERGAR swept into the lead and quickly drew away from his rivals. With his tongue swinging pendulously from the corner of his mouth, he passed the post four lengths clear of the filly Madam Gay who got up close home to deprive Fingal's Cave of second place. The early leader Light Cavalry finished in last position.

SHERGAR's success provided his sire Great Nephew with his second King George winner after Grundy's epic victory in 1975.

Somewhat surprisingly, connections announced that SHERGAR's

next race would be in the St Leger. The St Leger has become something of an "unfashionable" race in recent years, SHERGAR being the first Derby winner to contest the race since Nijinsky in 1970. In the event, he failed to stay the fourteen furlongs and 127 yards at Doncaster, trailing in fourth, over eleven lengths behind the winner Cut Above, a turn-around of over fifteen lengths on Irish Sweeps Derby running.

The St Leger proved to be SHERGAR's final race. Syndicated at a value of £10 million, he took up his stallion duties at the Aga Khan's Ballymany Stud in County Kildare. Then in one of the most amazing incidents in Turf history, SHERGAR was kidnapped by an armed gang on February 8, 1983. Clearly believing that the horse was still entirely the personal property of the Aga Khan, the culprits, a group from the lower echelons of the IRA, demanded a £2,000,000 ransom for the stallion.

Even if they had been unanimous in wishing to meet the gang's demands, shareholders had a moral responsibility to withhold payment. The whole future of the bloodstock industry in the British Isles was at stake. Any concession would have opened the way for other terrorist groups to fill their coffers. Sadly, it is believed that once the gang realised that the ransom would not be forthcoming, the 1981 "Horse of the Year" was unceremoniously murdered, a victim of his own brilliance.

SHERGAR's untimely death was a disaster for British racing since all available evidence suggests that he would have made a top-class stallion. During his one season at stud, SHERGAR managed to get thirty-six of his forty-four mares in foal. The best of his solitary crop were the 540,000 guineas yearling filly Maysoon who was placed in both the 1986 One Thousand Guineas and the Oaks, and the 1986 Irish St Leger winner Authaal.

# 1981

## KING GEORGE VI AND QUEEN ELIZABETH DIAMOND STAKES (GROUP ONE)

£119,206    1m 4f

July 25, 1981

| | | | |
|---|---|---|---|
| 1 SHERGAR | 3 8–8 | W. Swinburn. b.c. by Great Nephew–Sharmeen |
| 2 MADAM GAY | 3 8–6 | G. Starkey. b.f. by Star Appeal–Saucy Flirt |
| 3 FINGAL'S CAVE | 4 9–7 | P. Eddery. b.c. by Ragstone–Blue Echoes |
| 4 MASTER WILLIE | 4 9–7 | P. Waldron. ch.c. by High Line–Fair Winter |
| 5 PELERIN (FR) | 4 9–7 | B. Taylor. b.c. by Sir Gaylord–Padrona |
| 6 CRACAVAL | 5 9–7 | S. Cauthen. ch.h. by Mount Hagen–Priddy Maid |
| 7 LIGHT CAVALRY | 4 9–7 | L. Piggott. b.c. by Brigadier Gerard–Glass Slipper |

7 Ran

Going – Good to Firm

Distances: 4,sht hd,4,2½,sht hd,3

Time: 2:35.40

S.P. 2–5 SHERGAR, 7–1 MASTER WILLIE, 15–2 PELERIN, 12–1 LIGHT CAVALRY, 40–1 MADAM GAY, FINGAL'S CAVE, 80–1 CRACAVAL

Winner trained by Michael Stoute at Newmarket: owned by H. H. Aga Khan: bred by owner

Timeform rating of winner 140

# 1982

W hen it comes to unearthing bargain-priced embryonic champions from doorstep-thick sales catalogues, trainer Guy Harwood and bloodstock agent James Delahooke are "the business". Amongst the dynamic duo's more celebrated sales "steals" are Ela-Mana-Mou (4,500 guineas), Young Generation (9,000 guineas) and the 1982 King George winner KALAGLOW, who fetched just 11,500 guineas as a yearling. Such shrewd purchases were all the more remarkable in a period when yearling prices were still outrageously inflated on both sides of the Atlantic.

A grey son of Kalamoun, KALAGLOW initially raced in the colours of Mr J. T. Vanner. Rather on the leg at two, he nevertheless ended his first season the unbeaten winner of five races. After convincing victories at Newmarket, Sandown, Newbury and Goodwood, he scored his most important success in the Group Three Horris Hill Stakes, beating Major Hern's Cut Above by three parts of a length.

After a winter's break, the winning run continued in the Heath Stakes at Newmarket where KALAGLOW made all to beat Clear Verdict by four lengths. The grey was beginning to look like a Classic contender and connections set about planning his Derby preparation.

The Mecca Dante Stakes at York was chosen as the colt's final race before Epsom. But the bubble burst on the Knavesmire when KALAGLOW was beaten for the first time in his life, trailing home fifth of the six runners over fourteen lengths behind the winner, Beldale Flutter. There were no post-race excuses from the Harwood camp; the horse had simply run a bad race. Despite his dismal display in the Mecca Dante, KALAGLOW attracted plenty of support at Epsom and was sent off the third favourite behind Shergar and Lester Piggott's mount, Shotgun.

Some horses are born unlucky, others have misfortune thrust upon them, KALAGLOW fell into the latter category. After covering just four furlongs, the grey was badly struck into and his season was over. While the watching millions cheered home the mighty Shergar, a rather pathetic-looking KALAGLOW was hobbling his way to the racecourse stables.

After undergoing surgery, KALAGLOW made a full recovery and returned to Pulborough to prepare for the 1982 season. During the winter, a syndicate headed by Guy Harwood made a successful bid to purchase a half share in the colt from Mr Vanner, with the result that for the remainder of his racing career KALAGLOW carried the green and orange colours of syndicate member Tony Ward.

The grey returned to the track in the Earl of Sefton Stakes at Newmarket in April where he showed all his old sparkle in slamming Ring The Bell by three lengths. KALAGLOW stepped up in class for his next race, the Group One Prix Ganay at Longchamp. Taking on some of the best middle-distance horses in Europe, he was far from disgraced in finishing a close-up sixth behind the 1981 Prix du Jockey Club winner Bikala.

Some horses are well past their best by the age of four, but KALAGLOW was still improving. Proof came at Sandown at the end of May, when the son of Kalamoun gained his first Group One success in the Brigadier Gerard Stakes, smashing the course record in the process. After a month's rest, he returned to the scene of his record-breaking triumph with a scintillating four-length success in the Coral Eclipse Stakes. The colt was on a roll, and after the race a confident Guy Harwood announced that the next target for his stable star would be the King George at Ascot.

While KALAGLOW was sweeping all before him in England, another bargain buy, the David O'Brien-trained Assert, was gaining a lofty reputation in both Ireland and France. A £16,000 yearling, the son of Be My Guest, followed up an easy win in the Gallinule Stakes at the Curragh with a brilliant three-length success in the Prix du Jockey Club thus becoming the first ever foreign-trained winner of the French Derby. Robert Sangster's colt entered the record books for a second time when running away with the Irish Sweeps Derby by a staggering eight lengths. The King George promised the fascinating prospect of a clash between Assert, the dual Classic winner, and the season's leading four-year-old, KALAGLOW.

However, with horses of the calibre of Grand Prix de Paris winner Glint of Gold, Assert's half-brother Bikala and Major Hern's smart filly Height of Fashion in the field, the two market leaders would not have things all their own way at Ascot.

Diamond Day duly arrived and a tremendous crowd flocked to the Berkshire track to witness what promised to be the race of the season. KALAGLOW looked magnificent in the paddock, strolling around as if he owned the place. Assert too looked ready to run for his life, drawing admiring glances from racegoers packed ten deep around the leafy parade ring.

The nine-strong field reached the start without incident and were quickly loaded up by the stalls handlers. As the gates flashed open Height of Fashion was caught flat-footed and was left half a dozen lengths. The filly, recently purchased from the Queen by Sheikh Hamdan Al-Maktoum for a reputed £1.5 million, never recovered from her lapse of concentration and trailed the field throughout the race.

The French challenger Bikala was pushed into the lead by young Serge Gorli, a position he retained until well into the home straight. So strong was the pace set by the leader, that Lafontaine, normally a frontrunner, struggled in vain to match strides. Turning for home, Bikala still held the lead, but Lafontaine was beginning to feel the strain and quickly surrendered his position to the improving Assert. Greville Starkey had kept the Irish horse in his sights throughout and lost no time in sending KALAGLOW after the favourite. Two furlongs out, Bikala dropped out of contention as Assert, KALAGLOW, and Glint of Gold all made their bids for glory. Assert had first run on his rivals and looked full of running at the head of affairs. Starkey, however, still had plenty of horse under him and had no intention of letting the Diamonds cross the Irish Sea.

Race riding is all about making split-second decisions and the veteran jockey was about to have his judgement severely tested. As KALAGLOW went for a space between Assert and Glint of Gold, the gap closed and Starkey found himself with nowhere to go. In an instant he switched the grey onto the far rails, a manoeuvre which almost certainly won him the race. At the furlong marker Assert still looked the winner, but KALAGLOW, having at last found daylight, came with a sweeping run which enabled him to grasp the lead inside the final hundred yards. Assert rallied bravely under Christy

Roche's strong driving and the issue was not resolved until the very last strides. In one of the tightest finishes in the history of the race, KALAGLOW stuck his grey neck out on the line to snatch the prize from his Irish rival, the pair finishing three lengths clear of the ultraconsistent Glint of Gold. The 11,500 guineas yearling had beaten the £16,000 yearling to land the richest prize in British racing, proving that the "bargain basement" can still throw up a champion every now and then.

KALAGLOW ended his racing career in the Champion Stakes at Newmarket, where he looked all over the winner until being badly hampered just below the distance, eventually finishing an unlucky eighth of fourteen behind Time Charter.

After being syndicated at an estimated value of £5 million, KALAGLOW retired to the Brook Stud in Newmarket where he has made a promising start to his stallion career. Amongst his more talented offspring are the Group race winners, Knockando, Shining Water and Red Glow. Ironically, it is KALAGLOW's King George victim Height of Fashion who has made the greater impact on the bloodstock industry, having established herself as one of the greatest brood mares of the twentieth century with her three celebrated offspring, Alwasmi, Unfuwain, and the champion of 1989, Nashwan.

# 1982

## KING GEORGE VI AND QUEEN ELIZABETH DIAMOND STAKES (GROUP ONE)

£126,472.20     1m 4f

July 24, 1982

| | | | |
|---|---|---|---|
| 1 KALAGLOW | 4 | 9–7 | G. Starkey. gr.c. by Kalamoun–Rossitor |
| 2 ASSERT | 3 | 8–8 | C. Roche. b.c. by Be My Guest–Irish Bird |
| 3 GLINT OF GOLD | 4 | 9–7 | P. Eddery. b.c. by Mill Reef–Crown Treasure |
| 4 CRITIQUE (USA) | 4 | 9–7 | L. Piggott. br.c. by Roberto–Cambrienne |
| 5 BIKALA | 4 | 9–7 | S. Gorli. b.c. by Kalamoun–Irish Bird |
| 6 EASTER SUN | 5 | 9–7 | B. Raymond. b.h. by Bustino–Magical |
| 7 HEIGHT OF FASHION (FR) (b) | 3 | 8–5 | W. Carson. b.f. by Bustino–Highclere |
| 8 LAFONTAINE (USA) | 5 | 9–7 | S. Cauthen. b.h. by Sham–Valya |
| 9 DRONACHARYA (USA) | 6 | 9–7 | J. Mercer. gr. h. by Nijinsky–Belle de Nuit |

9 Ran

Going – Good to Firm

Distances: nk,3,nk,nk,10,8

Time: 2:31.88

S.P. 10–11 ASSERT, 11–12 BIKALA, 13–2 KALAGLOW, 9–1 HEIGHT OF FASHION, 10–1 GLINT OF GOLD, 13–1 CRITIQUE, EASTER SUN, 100–1 LAFONTAINE, 750–1 DRONACHARYA

Winner trained by Guy Harwood at Pulborough: owned by Mr A. Ward: bred by Someries Stud

Timeform rating of winner 132

# 1983

TIME CHARTER, the winner of the 1983 King George, possessed the ideal combination of speed and stamina which made her perfectly suited to middle distances. Her sire, Saritamer, winner of both the Cork and Orrery and the July Cup, provided the pace while the staying power came from the dam, Centrocon, victorious in the 1976 Lancashire Oaks. A strong, well-made filly, TIME CHARTER had scored twice as a juvenile without causing any particular excitement.

Trained by Henry Candy, she improved out of all recognition during her second season on the track. After finishing second to On The House in the 1982 One Thousand Guineas, TIME CHARTER went on to make history in the Oaks, beating Slightly Dangerous by a length in an exceptionally fast time. She thus provided Candy with his first Classic winner and made Billy Newnes the first apprentice to ride an Oaks winner since Joe Mercer had partnered Ambiguity to victory in 1953.

After a defeat by Dancing Rocks in the Nassau Stakes at Goodwood, TIME CHARTER ended her season with wins in the Sun Chariot Stakes and in the Dubai Champion Stakes where she beat Prima Voce by seven lengths. Unfortunately a combination of an internal abscess and extremely bad weather in the spring of 1983 meant TIME CHARTER was on the easy list during the early part of her four-year-old season. By the time she lined up for the King George in July, TIME CHARTER had been beaten in both the Jockey Club Stakes and the Coral Eclipse Stakes. In the former she had clearly not come in her coat and went under by a head to Stoute's Electric. In the latter, she was given far too much to do by Newnes. Last of the nine runners with two furlongs to run the filly made rapid headway in the closing stages to finish sixth behind Solford.

Fate decided that Newnes would not be aboard TIME CHARTER at Ascot. Nine days before the race the Liverpool-born jockey came close to death having been pinned down by his mount Silver Venture on the gallops. Thanks to the kiss of life Newnes recovered, but was not fit to ride in the King George and the mount on TIME CHARTER went to the veteran Joe Mercer who had partnered the legendary Brigadier Gerard to victory in 1972.

The 1983 field was well above average. After the Aga Khan's Khairpour had been withdrawn at the start having cut his leg after being stung by a wasp, the field was reduced to nine. The main dangers to TIME CHARTER were Diamond Shoal, Sun Princess, and Caerleon.

The four-year-old Diamond Shoal, a full brother to Glint of Gold, had won four races since the start of the season. After taking the John Porter Stakes, he went on to win three races abroad, the Grand Prix d'Evry, the Gran Premio di Milano and the Grand Prix de Saint-Cloud.

Sun Princess had become the first maiden to win an English Classic for thirty-three years when she landed the Oaks by an amazing twelve lengths. By English Prince out of a Val de Loir mare, Major Hern's filly would be staying on up the Ascot straight when many of her opponents had run out of steam.

Caerleon, trained by the peerless Vincent O'Brien, had beaten the best of the French-trained three-year-old colts on their own soil in the Prix du Jockey Club. After his three-length success over L'Emigrant, Caerleon was unlucky in running when beaten three lengths by Shareef Dancer in the Irish Sweeps Derby.

The ex-American Lemhi Gold was an interesting candidate. The Vaguely Noble five-year-old had won an Eclipse Award as Champion Handicap Male in 1982 after winning six races in America. Now trained by Douieb in France, the chestnut was something of a "dark horse".

From the break Lemhi Gold and Diamond Shoal made the running, closely followed by Lancastrian and Awaasif. At the rear of the field Mercer held TIME CHARTER up for a late run. The order hardly changed until two furlongs from home, where Diamond Shoal forged into a two-length lead. Mercer immediately saw the danger and set about rousing his filly.

At the furlong marker the contest had developed into a two-horse race, only TIME CHARTER having any chance of catching Diamond Shoal. Coming with an irresistible run on the outside, the filly hit the front 150 yards out, pulling away from her rival to win cleverly by three quarters of a length. A length behind Diamond Shoal came Sun Princess who had wasted valuable energy by fighting for her head throughout the race. Caerleon, who had lost both of his front plates during the race, finished last of the nine runners.

TIME CHARTER travelled to France for her next race, the Prix Foy. Over the Arc course and distance, she beat All Along by three-quarters of a length, giving the Wildenstein filly seven pounds. In her final outing of the season TIME CHARTER, clearly past her best, started favourite for the Arc, but could finish only fourth behind her old rival, All Along.

Kept in training as a five-year-old, TIME CHARTER added the Coronation Cup to her list of Group race victories, but failed to win a second King George, finishing fourth behind Teenoso in 1984.

A tough and consistent filly on the racecourse, she should prove to be a fine brood mare.

# 1983

## KING GEORGE VI AND QUEEN ELIZABETH DIAMOND STAKES (GROUP ONE)

£133,851    1m 4f

July 23, 1983

| | | | |
|---|---|---|---|
| 1 TIME CHARTER | 4 | 9–4 | J. Mercer. b.f. by Saritamer–Centrocon |
| 2 DIAMOND SHOAL | 4 | 9–7 | L. Piggott. b.c. by Mill Reef–Crown Treasure |
| 3 SUN PRINCESS | 3 | 8–5 | W. Carson. b.f. by English Prince–Sunny Valley |
| 4 AWAASIF (CAN) | 4 | 9–4 | B. Raymond. b.f. by Snow Knight–Royal Salute |
| 5 LANCASTRIAN | 6 | 9–7 | A. Lequeux. b.h. by Reform–Rosalie II |
| 6 CARLINGFORD CASTLE | 3 | 8–8 | G. Starkey. ch.c. by Le Bavard–Rachel Ruysch |
| 7 ROCAMADOUR (b) | 4 | 9–7 | B. Rouse, b.c. by Royal Match–Blakeney Belle |
| 8 LEMHI GOLD (USA) | 5 | 9–7 | F. Head. ch.h. by Vaguely Noble–Belle Marie |
| 9 CAERLEON (USA) | 3 | 8–8 | P. Eddery. b.c. by Nijinsky–Foreseer |

9 Ran

Going – Firm

Distances: ¾,1,2,5,3

Time: 2:30.79

S.P. 9–4 CAERLEON, SUN PRINCESS, 5–1 TIME CHARTER, 8–1 DIAMOND SHOAL, 15–1 AWAASIF, 16–1 LEMHI GOLD, 25–1 CARLINGFORD CASTLE, 33–1 LANCASTRIAN, 150–1 ROCAMADOUR

Winner trained by Henry Candy at Wantage: owned by Mr R. Barnett: bred by owner

Timeform rating of winner 130

# 1984

TEENOSO, the 1984 King George hero, had been dismissed by many "experts" as a substandard Derby winner. In putting a field of top-class performers in their place at Ascot, TEENOSO proved conclusively that his 1983 Epsom victory had been gained strictly on merit.

An imposing rangy colt by the 1976 Prix du Jockey Club winner Youth, he was bred by his owner Eric Moller from his Oaks runner-up Furioso, a descendant of the Moller brothers' foundation mare Horama. Furioso had previously produced the smart filly Topsy, who also carried the Mollers' chocolate and gold colours with distinction. Geoff Wragg, who took over from his father Harry in 1983, handled TEENOSO with considerable skill and patience.

As a two-year-old TEENOSO gave little indication of the heights he was to scale later in his career. From three starts the colt managed to trouble the judge only once, when fourth of seventeen in a maiden race at Newmarket.

The spring of 1983 was the wettest on record and the rain-softened ground brought about a vast improvement in TEENOSO's form. After landing a maiden race at Newmarket, Geoff Wragg sent TEENOSO to Lingfield to contest the Highland Spring Derby Trial. In testing conditions the son of Youth comfortably accounted for Shearwalk by three lengths.

For the first time in more than fifty years the going on Derby day was officially described as heavy and Piggott rode a masterful race on a horse he knew would revel in the sodden ground. Up with the pace throughout, he kicked TEENOSO into the lead early in the straight, the partnership crossing the line three lengths clear of Carlingford Castle.

But conditions were radically different at the Curragh on Irish

Sweeps Derby day. On firm going TEENOSO was beaten into third place by Shareef Dancer and Caerleon, and in his final race of the 1983 season, the Great Voltigeur Stakes, he sustained an off foreleg injury when third to Seymour Hicks. Initially it was feared that the injury would end TEENOSO's racing career, but under the watchful eye of Geoff Wragg and his team the colt recovered and remained in training as a four-year-old.

Eight months after his accident at York, TEENOSO reappeared in the John Porter Stakes where, under a sympathetic ride from Piggott, he ran a creditable third behind Gay Lemur.

After returning to winning ways in the Ormonde Stakes at Chester, TEENOSO crossed the English Channel to contest the Grand Prix de Saint-Cloud. He was attempting a hat trick for English-trained horses, Ian Balding having won the race with Glint of Gold in 1982 and with Diamond Shoal in 1983. Despite fast conditions and Piggott sustaining a nasty cut above his right eye when TEENOSO reared up in the parade ring, the English combination came home the victors by a short neck from the French horse Fly Me. TEENOSO's victory proved that although he preferred soft going, top-of-the-ground conditions held no terrors for him. Nevertheless, the racing public were still not fully convinced that he could beat the best horses in Europe on fast ground, and consequently sent him off only third favourite for the King George behind market leader, Time Charter.

Time Charter was attempting to win her second King George after her success twelve months earlier, a feat only previously achieved by the French filly Dahlia. A runaway success in the Coronation Cup confirmed that she had retained her ability as a five-year-old, although she appeared held by Sadler's Wells on their Coral Eclipse running.

Vincent O'Brien's Sadler's Wells had beaten Time Charter by a neck at Sandown and his connections were confident that the colt would confirm the form at Ascot. An impressive bay son of Northern Dancer, Sadler's Wells had a habit of racing with his head high in the air. This kink had not prevented the colt from winning the Arlie/Coolmore Irish Two Thousand Guineas and running a tremendous race in the Prix du Jockey Club where he finished a close second to Darshaan.

The Aga Khan's Darshaan, a son of Shirley Heights, had landed both the Prix Greffulhe and the Prix Hocquart prior to his French

Derby success and was strongly fancied to give the French their ninth King George. Tolomeo, hero of the 1983 Budweiser Million, and the 1983 King George third, Sun Princess, were also expected to run well.

A most unusual incident occurred prior to the start of the race. One of the French challengers, Esprit du Nord, had been declared to run in blinkers but arrived at the start without the aid. Trainer John Fellows had tried to fit the blinkers in the paddock but the horse had become fractious and Fellows decided to try again after the horse had cantered to the post. The Stewards, however, ruled that Fellows had contravened rule 147, and therefore Esprit du Nord was ineligible to run as he had arrived at the start with incorrect tack. An angry Fellows was fined £200.

As the stalls burst open, Piggott dashed TEENOSO straight into the lead. The pair had made such a flying start that Sun Princess's pacemaker, His Honour, took all of three furlongs to take the lead. Piggott settled his mount in second place, just ahead of Sun Princess, Sadler's Wells and Darshaan.

Half a mile from home TEENOSO regained the lead as His Honour ran out of steam. Rounding the home turn Piggott decided it was time to get serious. Under strong driving TEENOSO pulled two lengths clear of the chasing pack headed by Sun Princess. At the furlong marker the Hern filly had nothing left to give, leaving a triumvirate of Sadler's Wells, Tolomeo, and Time Charter as TEENOSO's only serious challengers.

Sadler's Wells proved the toughest of the trio, battling his way up to TEENOSO's quarters. Piggott's whip rose and fell repeatedly inside the last hundred yards, urging his mount to dig deep into his reserves. TEENOSO responded magnificently, extending his lead over the Irish challenger to two and a half lengths at the line. Tolomeo, who had run on strongly inside the final furlong without ever looking likely to trouble the two leaders, finished third ahead of the double-seeking Time Charter. The time, 2:27.95, was the second fastest in the history of the race, having been bettered only by the "Race of the Century" in 1975.

TEENOSO was made the ante-post favourite for the Arc, but an off foreleg injury prevented his participation, and he was retired to stand at the Highclere Stud in Berkshire. Unfortunately for his owners, TEENOSO's sire line has not proved commercially successful.

*Above:* 1974. DAHLIA makes light work of landing her second King George.
*Below:* 1975. GRUNDY and Pat Eddery snatch the verdict over BUSTINO in the 'race of the century'.

*Top left:* PAWNEESE, the 1976 heroine.
*Bottom left:* THE MINSTREL after his courageous victory in 1977.
*Top right:* Poetry in motion – TROY and Willie Carson.
*Bottom right:* 1980. Carson lands the Diamonds for the second successive year – this time aboard ELA-MANA-MOU.

*Top left:* The ill-fated SHERGAR destroys his rivals in 1981.
*Top centre:* Joe Mercer and TIME CHARTER are led in after beating DIAMOND SHOAL in 1983.
*Top right:* The imposing grey, KALAGLOW, going to post in 1982.
*Right:* 1984. The under-rated TEENOSO proves a point by beating the favourite SADLER'S WELLS by a comfortable two-and-a-half lengths.

*Above:* PETOSKI going to post in 1985.
*Below:* REFERENCE POINT and Steve Cauthen.
*Left:* DANCING BRAVE and Pat Eddery enter the winner's enclosure after their breath-taking victory in 1986.

*Above:* A winning combination – MTOTO and Michael Roberts.
*Below:* A blood-stirring finish as NASHWAN inches out CACOETHES to land the Diamonds in 1989.

Youth is currently an "unfashionable" sire, his yearlings not commanding the vast amounts which might be expected of the offspring of a Prix du Jockey Club winner. Sadly TEENOSO appears to be suffering the same fate as his sire. Given a reasonable chance, the 1984 King George winner might just prove the sceptics wrong.

## 1984

### KING GEORGE VI AND QUEEN ELIZABETH DIAMOND STAKES (GROUP ONE)

£141,247     1m 4f

July 28, 1984

| | | | |
|---|---|---|---|
| 1 | TEENOSO (USA) | 4 9–7 | L. Piggott. b.c. by Youth–Furioso |
| 2 | SADLER'S WELLS (USA) | 3 8–8 | P. Eddery. b.c. by Northern Dancer–Fairy Bridge |
| 3 | TOLOMEO | 4 9–7 | R. Guest. b.c. by Lypheor–Almagest |
| 4 | TIME CHARTER | 5 9–4 | J. Mercer. b.m. by Saritamer–Centrocon |
| 5 | SUN PRINCESS | 4 9–4 | S. Cauthen. b.f. by English Prince–Sunny Valley |
| 6 | JUPITER ISLAND | 5 9–7 | P. Robinson. b.h. by St Paddy–Mrs Moss |
| 7 | DAHAR (USA) | 3 8–8 | A. Lequeur. b.c. by Lyphard–Dahlia |
| 8 | LUTH ENCHANTÉE (FR) | 4 9–4 | M. Philipperon. ch.f. by Be My Guest–Viole d'Amour |
| 9 | FLY ME (FR) | 4 9–4 | F. Head. ch.f. by Luthier–On The Wing |
| 10 | DARSHAAN | 3 8–8 | W. Swinburn. br.c. by Shirley Heights–Delsy |
| 11 | MAGWAL (FR) | 5 9–7 | G. Starkey. b.h. by Dictus–Val Gardena |
| 12 | MIRAMAR REEF | 5 9–7 | R. Fox. b.h. by Mill Reef–Thalassa |
| 13 | HIS HONOUR | 4 9–7 | B. Procter. b.c. by Bustino–Honerko |

13 Ran

Going – Good to Firm

Distances: 2½,1½,2½,hd,2½,1

Time: 2:27.95

S.P. 6–4 TIME CHARTER, 9–2 DARSHAAN, 13–2 TEENOSO, 7–1 SADLER'S WELLS, 8–1 SUN PRINCESS, 12–1 LUTH ENCHANTÉE, 20–1 TOLOMEO, 25–1 FLY ME, 50–1 MAGWAL, JUPITER ISLAND, 66–1 DAHAR, 100–1 MIRAMAR REEF, 200–1 HIS HONOUR

Winner trained by G. Wragg at Newmarket: owned by Mr E. B. Moller: bred by owner in USA

Timeform rating of winner 135

# 1985

Henry Cecil had a remarkable season in 1985. Apart from the Ever Ready Derby winner Slip Anchor, his Warren Place stable also housed Oh So Sharp, winner of the fillies' Triple Crown. The King George however, remained elusively just beyond his grasp, one of the few Group One races the Newmarket trainer had failed to win. Cecil was denied his first King George by PETOSKI, trained by Major Hern.

PETOSKI was purchased for 90,000 guineas on behalf of Lady Beaverbrook at the 1983 Newmarket Sales. Lady Beaverbrook's beaver brown and maple leaf green colours had been carried to victory in the 1979 Irish St Leger by PETOSKI's sire Niniski.

A big, strong, rangy colt, PETOSKI was a top-class two-year-old who kept his connections well watered with victories in the Champagne Stakes at Salisbury and in the Lanson Champagne Stakes at Goodwood.

PETOSKI had four runs as a three-year-old prior to the King George. After finishing a close second to Damister in the Guardian Classic Trial, he filled the same position behind Law Society in the Dalham Chester Vase. A 33–1 chance at Epsom, PETOSKI ran like an outsider, finishing eleventh of thirteen behind Slip Anchor, Henry Cecil's first winner of the Blue Riband. Major Hern gave PETOSKI a month to recover after Epsom, the horse returning revitalised to notch up his first success of the season in the Princess of Wales Stakes at Newmarket. Brought with a strong run inside the final furlong by Willie Carson, PETOSKI beat Guy Harwood's Crazy by a comfortable two lengths. Believing that their colt was capable of significant improvement, PETOSKI's connections decided to take the bull by the horns and go for the King George.

Although Slip Anchor was prevented from running at Ascot due to a near fore injury, Cecil was able to field a super-sub in the shape of the filly Oh So Sharp. A most attractive chestnut filly from the first crop of Kris, Oh So Sharp had won all three of her races as a juvenile, culminating in a length and a half victory over Hern's Helen Street in the Hoover Fillies' Mile at Ascot. Sheikh Mohammed's filly started the 1985 season in the Nell Gwyn Stakes where she accounted for Bella Colora by a length. Two Classic victories followed. In the General Accident One Thousand Guineas she short-headed Al Bahathri after coming with a tremendous late run and at Epsom Oh So Sharp led two furlongs out in the Gold Seal Oaks, drawing clear of Triptych to win by a long-looking six lengths. Unbeaten in six races, Cecil's filly headed the King George market at 4–5.

Apart from Oh So Sharp there were four other Classic winners in the field – Law Society, winner of the Joe McGrath Irish Sweeps Derby, Princess Pati, successful in the 1984 Gilltown Stud Irish Oaks, the Australian Derby winner Strawberry Road and Sirius Symboli, winner of the Japanese Derby.

Although he had not won a Classic, Jeremy Tree's Blushing Groom colt Rainbow Quest also held sound claims. Raced in the highest class, Rainbow Quest had just missed out on Classic honours in 1984. As a four-year-old the colt had won his first two races, the Clive Graham Stakes and the Coronation Cup, before filling the runner's-up position behind Pebbles in the Coral Eclipse. In order to ensure a strong gallop for Rainbow Quest, Tree decided to run the four-year-old August in the King George as a pacemaker.

The 1985 King George proved to be one of the most exciting races run in Britain all season. The pacemaker August soon established a commanding lead. So strong was the gallop that the field was stretched out in Indian file by the halfway stage, with PETOSKI in ninth place, fully fifteen lengths behind the leader. Just before the home turn, Infantry, ridden by the Australian-based jockey Brent Thomson, moved into the lead, closely followed by Rainbow Quest and Oh So Sharp. At this stage Carson could be seen pumping away on PETOSKI back in sixth place.

Halfway up the straight Lady Beaverbrook's colt took hold of his bit and started to make rapid progress on the outside of the field. Inside the final furlong, Carson threw down his challenge to the two leaders, Oh So Sharp and Rainbow Quest. Rainbow Quest was the first to crack, leaving PETOSKI and Oh So Sharp to fight out the finish.

With Carson riding like a man possessed, PETOSKI inched ahead of his rival inside the last fifty yards. Although the filly fought courageously under Steve Cauthen, the colt maintained his advantage, crossing the line with a neck to spare. Rainbow Quest finished a gallant third, just ahead of Law Society, with the rest of the field well strung out.

PETOSKI's victory was made to look even more meritorious when Oh So Sharp beat the three-year-old colts in the St Leger to claim the fillies' Triple Crown and Rainbow Quest was awarded the Arc on the disqualification of Sagace.

But PETOSKI failed to show anything like his Ascot form in three races as a four-year-old, a second crack at the King George resulting in a disappointing sixth place behind the brilliant Dancing Brave.

PETOSKI may not have been the best horse to have won the King George, but in beating the Triple Crown winner Oh So Sharp he put up a performance of the highest class.

He stands at the National Stud in Newmarket.

# 1985

## KING GEORGE VI AND QUEEN ELIZABETH DIAMOND STAKES (GROUP ONE)

£134,274      1m 4f

July 27, 1985

| | | | |
|---|---|---|---|
| 1 PETOSKI | 3 8–8 | W. Carson. b.c. by Niniski–Sushila | |
| 2 OH SO SHARP | 3 8–5 | S. Cauthen. ch.f. by Kris–Oh So Fair | |
| 3 RAINBOW QUEST (USA) | 4 9–7 | W. Swinburn. b.c. by Blushing Groom–I Will Follow | |
| 4 LAW SOCIETY (USA) | 3 8–8 | P. Eddery. br.c. by Alleged–Bold Bikini | |
| 5 RAFT (USA) | 4 9–7 | G. Starkey. br.c. by Nodouble–Gangster of Love | |
| 6 STRAWBERRY ROAD (AUS) | 6 9–7 | Y. Saint-Martin, b.h. by Whiskey Road–Giftisa | |
| 7 INFANTRY | 3 8–8 | B. Thomson. ch.c. by Northfields–Princess Tiara | |
| 8 SIRIUS SYMBOLI (JAP) | 3 8–8 | Y. Okabe. b.c. by Mogami–Sweet Epsom | |
| 9 TREIZIEME (USA) | 4 9–4 | A. Lequeux. ch.f. by The Minstrel–Belle Pensee | |
| 10 CRAZY (FR) | 4 9–7 | L. Piggott. b.c. by Crystal Palace–Aunt Zara | |
| 11 PRINCESS PATI | 4 9–4 | P. Shanahan. b.f. by Top Ville–Sarah Siddons | |
| 12 AUGUST (USA) | 4 9–7 | S. Raymont. b.c. by Sensitive Prince–Polynesian Charm | |

12 Ran

Going – Firm

Distances: nk,¾,1½,1½,hd,4

Time: 2:27.61

S.P. 4–5 OH SO SHARP, 3–1 LAW SOCIETY, 12–1 RAINBOW QUEST, STRAWBERRY

ROAD, PETOSKI, 22—1 CRAZY, RAFT, 33—1 INFANTRY, 66—1 TREIZIEME, 100—1 SIRIUS SYMBOLI, PRINCESS PATI, 1000—1 AUGUST

Winner trained by Major Hern at West Ilsley: owned by Lady Beaverbrook: bred by Miss K. Rausing

Timeform rating of winner 135

# 1986

D ANCING BRAVE, the 1986 King George hero, was undoubtedly one of the finest racehorses to grace the Turf this century. Purchased for $200,000 as a yearling by Khaled Abdulla, the son of top-class miler Lyphard was unbeaten as a two-year-old, winning minor contests at Sandown and Newmarket. Although highly thought of by his trainer, Guy Harwood, DANCING BRAVE was rated eleven pounds behind stable companion Bakharoff in the Free Handicap.

Having wintered extremely well, DANCING BRAVE made his three-year-old debut at Newmarket in the Charles Heidsieck Champagne Craven Stakes and the Lyphard colt emerged from the race as a potential Guineas winner. In the hands of Greville Starkey, DANCING BRAVE made light work of beating the Henry Cecil-trained pair Faraway Dancer and Mashkour. Starting the 15–8 favourite in the Two Thousand Guineas, DANCING BRAVE put up a breathtaking performance to beat the useful Green Desert by three lengths. Guy Harwood's colt was immediately installed as Derby favourite.

On breeding DANCING BRAVE was not certain to stay the mile and a half at Epsom. His sire, Lyphard, failed to win beyond 10.5 furlongs and the majority of his offspring had proved to be milers. In addition, Lyphard had experienced difficulty in handling tight turns on the racecourse, his eccentric attempt at rounding Tattenham Corner in the 1972 Derby providing damning evidence of this weakness. Despite these doubts, both Harwood and Starkey were convinced DANCING BRAVE would win the Derby.

Without detracting from the merit of the winner, the 1986 Epsom Derby will go down in history as the race DANCING BRAVE lost rather than the one Shahrastani won. Turning into Tattenham Corner, Starkey had only two of his sixteen rivals behind him. Despite producing blistering speed in the home straight, DANCING BRAVE's late run failed by a rapidly diminishing half length. After the race Starkey was castigated by the press and public alike. How could such an experienced jockey have set his horse such a seemingly impossible task? In Starkey's defence, DANCING BRAVE's defeat was probably due to an inherent inability to handle the sharp Epsom turns, as well as his rider's exhibition of poor judgement. In the event, DANCING BRAVE must be considered one of the best horses never to have won the Derby.

Epsom at least proved that DANCING BRAVE stayed a mile and a half. For his next race, however, Harwood sent his colt to Sandown to tackle the mile and a quarter of the Coral Eclipse Stakes. In beating the ultra-game Triptych by four effortless lengths, DANCING BRAVE proved himself the best mile-and-a-quarter horse in Europe. The King George would give the son of Lyphard the chance to gain his revenge over his Epsom conqueror Shahrastani, and to claim the mile-and-a-half crown most observers felt he deserved. Harwood had landed the Eclipse–King George double with Kalaglow in 1982, now he was convinced DANCING BRAVE would repeat the feat.

Although geldings were eligible to run in the King George for the first time in 1986, none were declared to take on DANCING BRAVE and Shahrastani. The two principals dominated the market with the Stoute-trained horse just preferred at 11–10, with DANCING BRAVE at 6–4 and 14–1 bar the two. The Harwood horse had a new pilot, Pat Eddery, who replaced the injured Greville Starkey.

Shahrastani lined up for the big race the winner of all four of his three-year-old contests. After winning the Guardian Classic Trial, the Mecca Dante Stakes and the Epsom Derby, the Nijinsky colt had put up a most impressive performance to take the Budweiser Irish Derby by eight lengths from Bonhomie with DANCING BRAVE's stable companion Bakharoff a further length and a half back in third place. Connections expected their horse to uphold the Epsom result.

In addition to Shahrastani, the Aga Khan was also represented by Dihistan and Shardari, also trained by Michael Stoute. Shardari, winner of the Princess of Wales Stakes, was the more fancied of the two, Steve Cauthen taking the ride. Dihistan, winner of the Clive Graham Stakes and the Hardwicke Stakes, was allowed to start at 100–1.

Of the remainder, only the 1985 winner Petoski and the consistent

Triptych had the form to trouble the two market leaders. Lady Beaverbrook's Petoski had finished behind Triptych in the Coronation Cup, and behind Shardari in the Princess of Wales Stakes, and seemed to have only a remote chance of repeating his 1985 victory. But Triptych, winner of a Group III race at Longchamp on her previous racecourse appearance, could never be left out of calculations, especially during the summer and autumn months when she invariably ran her best races.

The other three runners had no chance of landing the prize. Boldden and Vouchsafe were to act as pacemakers for stablemate Petoski, and Supreme Leader was realistically priced at 150–1.

Down at the start, Shahrastani began to show signs of temperament, sweating heavily and refusing to go into the stalls. Appearing to have run up light behind the saddle, he tested the skill of the handlers before eventually consenting to be loaded. DANCING BRAVE, on the other hand, looked perfectly relaxed and went into his stall with the minimum of fuss.

From the break, Boldden and Vouchsafe set a furious pace. Eight lengths behind the leaders came the Stoute trio Dihistan, Shardari and Shahrastani. Keeping his main rival in his sights, Eddery settled DANCING BRAVE in behind the main bunch with only Triptych, who was finding the pace too hot, behind him. By the time the pacemakers reached Swinley Bottom they were ten lengths clear. In a matter of strides however, they had come back to the field as Dihistan took over the lead.

As Eddery began his move prior to the home turn, he met interference from the weakening Boldden and as Shardari and Shahrastani made the best of their way home, Eddery brought DANCING BRAVE out from the rails, brushing Petoski in the process.

Having obtained a clear run, DANCING BRAVE hit the front over a furlong out. Surprisingly the anticipated challenge did not come from Shahrastani who found nothing in the closing stages, but from the Aga Khan's second string Shardari. In the hands of Steve Cauthen the Top Ville colt rallied extremely gamely to run DANCING BRAVE to three-quarters of a length. Triptych, who had been outpaced in the early stages put in her best work at the finish, beating Shahrastani for third place. Swinburn had eased his mount once his chance had gone.

The time of 2:29.49 had been bettered only four times in the previous twenty runnings of the race and DANCING BRAVE had become the first colt since Nijinsky to complete the Two Thousand Guineas–King George double in the same season.

After the King George, Harwood announced that his champion would go to Longchamp for the Arc and that Pat Eddery would keep the ride. DANCING BRAVE won the Arc by an official one and a half lengths. The plain facts, however, do little justice to DANCING BRAVE's performance at Longchamp. In essence he destroyed the best Arc field assembled for over a decade in record time.

Connections decided to send their champion of Europe to take on the best of the Americans in the Breeders Cup Turf at Santa Anita. But DANCING BRAVE ran like a tired horse to finish a well-beaten fourth of nine behind the American-trained Manila, Theatrical and Estrapade. The effects of a long season, a tight course and jet lag combined to bring about a disappointing end to a golden season.

DANCING BRAVE was syndicated after his Eclipse victory at a reputed value of £14 million. He was retired to the Dalham Hall Stud in Newmarket, the winner of seven of his nine races.

DANCING BRAVE was a racehorse of the highest calibre. Performing with outstanding consistency from April to October on going ranging from soft to firm, he proved himself the undisputed champion of Europe at a mile, a mile and a quarter and a mile and a half.

In his first season at stud, DANCING BRAVE developed Marie's Disease which threatened to end his life. Happily he appears to have made a full recovery and his first progeny are eagerly awaited.

## 1986

### KING GEORGE VI AND QUEEN ELIZABETH DIAMOND STAKES (GROUP ONE)

£152,468      1m 4f

July 26, 1986

| | | |
|---|---|---|
| 1 DANCING BRAVE (USA) | 3 8–8 | P. Eddery. b.c. by Lyphard–Navajo Princess |
| 2 SHARDARI | 4 9–7 | S. Cauthen. b.c. by Top Ville–Sharmada |
| 3 TRIPTYCH (USA) | 4 9–4 | Y. Saint-Martin. b.f. by Riverman–Trillion |
| 4 SHAHRASTANI (USA) | 3 8–8 | W. Swinburn. ch.c. by Nijinsky– Shademah |
| 5 DIHISTAN | 4 9–7 | A. Kimberley. b.c. by Tyrnavos–Damosa |
| 6 PETOSKI | 4 9–7 | W. Carson. b.c. by Niniski–Sushila |
| 7 SUPREME LEADER | 4 9–7 | A. Murray. b.c. by Bustino–Princess Zena |
| 8 VOUCHSAFE | 4 9–7 | B. Procter. b.c. by Bustino– Gracious-Consent |
| 9 BOLDDEN | 4 9–7 | P. Cook. b.c. by Bold Lad–Golden Keep |

9 Ran

Going – Good

Distances: ¾,4,5,2,1½

Time: 2:29.49

S.P. 11–10 SHAHRASTANI, 6–4 DANCING BRAVE, 14–1 SHARDARI, PETOSKI, 25–1 TRIPTYCH, 100–1 DIHISTAN, 150–1 SUPREME LEADER, 1000–1 VOUCH-SAFE, BOLDDEN

Winner trained by G. Harwood at Pulborough: owned by Mr K. Abdulla: bred by Glen Oak Farm in USA

Timeform rating of winner 140

# 1987

The entire racing world was dealt a colossal blow when Mill Reef, the 1971 King George winner, was put down on humanitarian grounds at the age of eighteen on February 2, 1986. Paul Mellon's colt had proved himself a stallion of the highest calibre with produce like Shirley Heights, Acamas, Glint of Gold, Diamond Shoal and Fairy Footsteps. Although Acamas sadly proved to be infertile, the Mill Reef dynasty should continue to flourish through his many sons who have taken up stallion duties around the world; indeed Shirley Heights has already produced the 1985 Derby winner Slip Anchor. Arguably, however, the best colt sired by Mill Reef was the 1987 "Racehorse of the Year" REFERENCE POINT.

In an industry increasingly dominated by Arab wealth, REFERENCE POINT was that sadly rare phenomenon, a champion owned, bred and trained in England – almost an endangered species. Owner Louis Freedman bred REFERENCE POINT from his Habitat mare Home On The Range, winner of the Sun Chariot Stakes in 1981. Freedman had previously owned such high-class animals at Attica Meli and Polygamy.

Although he was never spectacular on the gallops, the Newmarket dogs were barking the name of REFERENCE POINT even before he made his racecourse debut in the E. B. F. Heart of Variety Stakes at Sandown Park. After making steady headway in the closing stages, the Henry Cecil-trained colt finished a promising third behind the more experienced Port Hélène. He contested two more races as a two-year-old. After strolling home in the Dorking Stakes, he put up a tremendous performance in the William Hill Futurity at Doncaster. Forcing the pace from the start, REFERENCE POINT left his opponents toiling in his wake, drawing away for an effortless victory. The official winning margin was announced as five lengths, but in reality it was closer to seven. Pat Eddery was the fortunate pilot, stable jockey Steve Cauthen having chosen to partner Suhailie who finished a disappointing seventh.

His Doncaster victory took REFERENCE POINT to the top of the Free Handicap, two pounds ahead of the Dewhurst winner Ajdal and the filly Forest Flower. With plenty of scope for physical development, Louis Freedman's colt went into winter quarters as a live Derby prospect, despite the fact that the top-rated juvenile had not gone on to win the Epsom Classic since Grundy in 1975.

Those with ante-post Derby vouchers appeared to have burnt their fingers when Henry Cecil announced that REFERENCE POINT had developed a serious sinus problem which would necessitate surgery. The operation meant drilling a hole through the horse's head into which tubes were inserted to allow the sinuses to be drained. Afterwards, REFERENCE POINT was prescribed a five-week course of antibiotics and a long period of convalescence. Although the operation proved successful, the antibiotics produced a reaction which led to the development of a cyst inside the nose, further delaying a return to the racecourse.

Just three weeks before the Derby, REFERENCE POINT made his seasonal debut in the Mecca Dante Stakes at York. Although only eighty per cent fit, he made all under Steve Cauthen to beat the highly regarded Ascot Knight by a length. The Derby was still within reach. All around the country punters were frantically searching through their dustbins for discarded ante-post vouchers.

REFERENCE POINT slaughtered his opponents at Epsom, making all the running to beat Most Welcome by a length and a half, in a time only 0.59 seconds outside Bustino's course record. Henry Cecil's race against time had been won in spectacular style.

On his only other appearance prior to the King George, REFERENCE POINT was caught inside the final furlong by Mtoto in the Eclipse Stakes at Sandown, going under by three-quarters of a length. In retrospect, Cecil's colt, who ideally needed twelve furlongs, lost nothing in defeat behind the 1988 "Racehorse of the Year".

Like many sons of Mill Reef, REFERENCE POINT was ideally suited by some give in the ground, conditions not always guaranteed at Ascot in July. Indeed, the King George had not been contested on soft going since 1957. As compensation for the setbacks experienced earlier in the season, the gods deemed it only fitting that REFERENCE POINT should have conditions in his favour, and contrived to produce the easy surface he required. The going would put a premium on stamina, REFERENCE POINT would revel in the conditions while some of his opponents would find twelve furlongs on testing ground beyond them.

The 1987 King George field was made up from the winners of twenty Group One races. In addition to REFERENCE POINT, the Classic generation was represented by the fillies Unite and Bourbon Girl and by the Barry Hills-trained colt Sir Harry Lewis. Unite, a rather angular Kris filly, was a dual Classic winner having accounted for Bourbon Girl in both the Gold Seal Oaks and the Giltown Stud Irish Oaks. Sir Harry Lewis also arrived at Ascot with a Classic victory under his belt. After upsetting the odds laid on Shady Heights in the Dee Stakes at Chester, the Alleged colt had scored a memorable victory over Naheez in the Budweiser Irish Derby.

Luca Cumani's four-year-old Celestial Storm was fancied by many to give his Italian trainer a first King George. The 1986 St Leger runner-up made a deep impression when breaking the Newmarket twelve-furlong course record in the Princess of Wales Stakes two weeks before Ascot.

John Dunlop's Moon Madness had beaten Celestial Storm in the final Classic of 1986 and had continued his winning ways in 1987 with a length-and-a-half victory over the Italian-trained Tony Bin in the Grand Prix de Saint-Cloud. Luigi Camici's colt appeared safely held on that form and was friendless in the market at 100-1.

The remarkable Triptych, third behind Dancing Brave in 1986, seemed as good as ever with victories in the Prix Ganay and the Coronation Cup to her credit. She had, however, finished behind REFERENCE POINT in the Eclipse and would be inconvenienced by the soft ground. The German Derby winner Acatenango, now a five-year-old, had suffered defeat at the hands of Triptych in the Coronation Cup and did not appear good enough to trouble the market leaders.

Steve Cauthen is probably the greatest exponent of the tactic of waiting in front. The American's riding of REFERENCE POINT at Ascot was simply masterly. Driving his mount straight into the lead from the break, Cauthen soon had his opponents struggling. Even before the halfway point Sir Harry Lewis and Bourbon Girl were flat to the boards.

Quickening the pace on the home turn, REFERENCE POINT held a two-length advantage over Acatenango, with Celestial Storm and Triptych the only other challengers. At this point Celestial Storm was checked in his run by the faltering Sir Harry Lewis.

At the two furlong marker, REFERENCE POINT had extended his lead to three lengths. As Acatenango began to weaken, however, Triptych, and Celestial Storm, who had switched from his position on the rails, started to reduce the favourite's lead. With a hundred yards to run Cauthen called for a supreme effort from his mount. REFERENCE POINT responded immediately, regaining his three-length advantage and maintaining it to the line. Celestial Storm held onto second with Triptych third for the second successive year. It later transpired that Unite, who had never been seen with a chance, had broken a blood vessel.

REFERENCE POINT had turned in the best performance by any horse all season, giving Henry Cecil and Steve Cauthen a first taste of King George success.

He raced on three further occasions after Ascot. After easily landing odds of 14–1 on in the Great Voltigeur, he won his second Classic of the season with a smooth victory over Mountain Kingdom in the Holsten Pils St Leger.

The colt's final appearance came in the Arc, where, after setting a scorching gallop, he dropped out in the straight in some distress and finished eighth behind Trempolino. Initially it was feared he had sustained a hairline fracture of the foreleg, but fortunately the problem was diagnosed as a burst abscess.

A strong, compact individual, REFERENCE POINT raced with an enthusiasm that was a pleasure to witness. He helped Cecil to rewrite the record books in 1987. With 180 winners the master of Warren Place shattered John Day's 120-year-old record, recording a phenomenal 40.4 per cent strike rate in the process.

Only the third horse to win the Derby, the King George and the St Leger, REFERENCE POINT retired to Dalham Hall Stud garlanded "Racehorse of the Year".

## 1987

## KING GEORGE VI AND QUEEN ELIZABETH DIAMOND STAKES (GROUP ONE)

£182,790    1m 4f

July 25, 1987

| 1 | REFERENCE POINT | 3 8–8 | S. Cauthen. b.c. by Mill Reef–Home On The Range |
| 2 | CELESTIAL STORM (USA) | 4 9–7 | R. Cochrane. b.c. by Roberto–Tobira Celeste |
| 3 | TRIPTYCH (USA) | 5 9–4 | A. Cruz. b.m. by Riverman–Trillion |
| 4 | MOON MADNESS | 4 9–7 | T. Ives. b.c. by Vitiges–Castle Moon |
| 5 | TONY BIN | 4 9–7 | M. Jerome. b.c. by Kampala–Severn Bridge |
| 6 | ACATENANGO (GER) | 5 9–7 | C. Asmussen. ch.h. by Surumu–Aggravate |
| 7 | SIR HARRY LEWIS (USA) | 3 8–8 | J. Reid. b.c. by Alleged–Sue Babe |
| 8 | UNITE | 3 8–6 | W. Swinburn. ch.f. by Kris–Pro Patria |
| 9 | BOURBON GIRL | 3 8–5 | P. Eddery. b.f. by Ile de Bourbon–Fleet Girl |

9 Ran

Going – Soft

Distances: 3,nk,5,hd,¾

Time: 2:34.63

S.P. 11–10 REFERENCE POINT, 5–1 CELESTIAL STORM, TRIPTYCH, 13–2 UNITE, 10–1 SIR HENRY LEWIS, 18–1 ACATENANGO, 25–1 MOON MADNESS, 40–1 BOURBON GIRL, 100–1 TONY BIN

Winner trained by Henry Cecil at Newmarket: owned by Mr Louis Freedman: bred by owner

Timeform rating of winner 139

# 1988

The name Harry Buckle may not mean much to most race-goers, but without his skill and expertise MTOTO would not have won the thirty-eighth King George. While trainer Alec Stewart, Jockey Michael Roberts and owner Sheikh Ahmed Al Maktoum were very much in the public eye throughout the 1988 season, blacksmith Harry Buckle remained almost totally anonymous.

Purchased as a yearling for 110,000 guineas, MTOTO needed plenty of time to realise his potential. By the 1967 King George winner Busted, he was brought along with extreme patience by his young trainer. The strapping bay ran only once as a juvenile, contesting a maiden at Yarmouth. Although never appearing likely to win, MTOTO ran on well in the closing stages to finish a respectable third at 20–1.

It was after the Yarmouth race that Stewart's troubles began. MTOTO chipped a bone in his near hind which necessitated intensive treatment. If this were not bad enough, Stewart then discovered that MTOTO's feet had become extremely brittle and had in fact stopped growing. No foot – no horse. Enter Harry Buckle. The role of the blacksmith is perhaps underrated by the racegoing public but certainly Buckle's contribution to the MTOTO story should not be understated. Every time MTOTO contested a race Buckle was on hand to tend those fragile hooves.

Sheikh Ahmed Al Maktoum's horse lost his maiden tag in a small race at Haydock in the June of his second season. Although he failed to add to his Haydock win, MTOTO ran with credit in each of his remaining races as a three-year-old, his best effort being a close fourth to Sure Blade in the Queen Elizabeth II Stakes at Ascot.

Like his sire, MTOTO improved rapidly from three to four. In his first race of 1987, the Brigadier Gerard Stakes at Sandown Park, he came with a beautifully timed late run under Michael Roberts to beat the highly regarded Allez Milord by two and a half lengths. MTOTO won his next race, the Prince of Wales Stakes by the same distance. The big horse was on a roll, and he notched up his hat trick of Group race victories in the Coral Eclipse. In his best performance of the season, MTOTO beat the 1987 Derby winner Reference Point by a hard fought three parts of a length after an epic battle up the home straight. Harry Buckle was certainly earning his keep.

Alec Stewart decided not to risk MTOTO in the 1987 King George due to the soft going, leaving Reference Point to take the Diamonds. Instead MTOTO went to Longchamp in October, where he ran a tremendous race in the Arc, finishing fourth behind Trempolino. The son of Busted ended his four-year-old campaign with his worst performance of the season, a disappointing eighth of eleven behind the remarkable Triptych in the Champion Stakes.

MTOTO's first race of 1988 proved to be something of a farce. In the Festival Stakes at Goodwood, the entire field took the wrong course after following incorrectly placed dolls. MTOTO won the race which was later declared void.

There were no such problems at Ascot in June, where MTOTO recorded his first "legal" victory of the season in the Prince of Wales Stakes. MTOTO then went on to Sandown where, for the second year in succession, he landed the Coral Eclipse. In beating Shady Heights by a neck, he became the first horse to do the double since Polyphontes in the twenties and he was clearly ready for the King George. Although he had never won over twelve furlongs, MTOTO's pedigree suggested he should have no problem getting the trip.

Even without the injured 1988 dual Derby winner Kahyasi, the Ascot showpiece attracted its usual glittering array of equine talent. With heavy overnight showers changing the going to good to soft, Major Hern's Unfuwain deposed MTOTO as market leader. Impeccably bred by Northern Dancer out of Height of Fashion, Unfuwain had won three of his four races prior to the King George. After emphatic victories in the Warren Stakes and the Dalham Chester Vase, Hamdam Al Maktoum's colt had disappointed in the Derby, finishing a poor seventh behind Kahyasi. In recording a runaway fifteen-length victory in the Princess of Wales Stakes, Unfuwain proved his Derby run was not his true form, and suggested he had a fine chance of landing the King George.

Michael Stoute, successful with Shergar in 1981, also fancied his chances of carrying off the Diamonds. Stoute's candidate, the Mill Reef colt Doyoun, had won the Two Thousand Guineas back in April. Many observers believed the colt would not stay twelve furlongs, but Doyoun proved his critics wrong with a gallant third in the Derby. The King George would be the three-year-old's first race against older horses.

The five-year-olds, Tony Bin and Almaarad were hardened campaigners, who were sure to make the younger horses fight all the way. The Italian-trained Tony Bin had been an unconsidered 100–1 chance in the 1987 King George, but returned to Ascot the well-supported third favourite at 9–2, a position earned with three top-class victories in Italy earlier in the season. He looked a good bet to improve on his fifth place in 1987. Almaarad, trained at Arundel by John Dunlop, had run consistently in top company prior to the King George. With emphatic successes in the Jockey Club Stakes and the Hardwicke Stakes to his credit, the Ela-Mana-Mou colt was well supported to upset the market leaders.

The temperamental Percy's Lass had earned the dreaded squiggle from Timeform and looked to have it all to do in such esteemed company. The same applied to the seemingly one-paced Derby runner-up Glacial Storm, the five-year-old Moon Madness and the French pair Soft Machine and Silver Lane.

As usual South African Michael Roberts planned to settle MTOTO at the rear of the field in the early stages of the race. With nobody eager to make the running, the pace was extremely slow, as Glacial Storm found himself leading on sufferance. A slow gallop was the last thing Roberts needed as he sought to restrain his enthusiastic mount.

At the halfway stage the pace had hardly increased, Glacial Storm still leading from Unfuwain, Doyoun, and Percy's Lass. Five furlongs out the lead changed as Moon Madness moved past Glacial Storm. But still the pace was slow. With three furlongs to run, the race began in earnest, with Unfuwain, Almaarad, Doyoun and MTOTO all starting their challenges.

Doyoun was the first to crack, weakening over a furlong out. Ahead of him Unfuwain and MTOTO had brushed aside Moon Madness and were engaged in a rousing struggle. In behind the two

[ 173 ]

Arab-owned horses, Tony Bin was making ground hand over fist. With a furlong to go MTOTO's white face inched ahead of Unfuwain, the pair maintaining their advantage over Tony Bin whose run had been short-lived. Under powerful driving from Roberts, MTOTO produced a dazzling burst of acceleration which took him two lengths clear of Carson's mount, an advantage maintained to the wire. MTOTO had become only the third five-year-old to win the race.

As Michael Roberts gave his famous victory wave to the Ascot crowd, it was announced that at 2:37.33 it had been the slowest King George since 1961, over ten seconds outside Grundy's record time.

MTOTO started favourite for the Arc on the strength of his Ascot victory. After being impeded several times in the home straight, he narrowly failed to catch Tony Bin, going under by a neck. As he had beaten the Italian-trained horse by three and a half lengths in the King George, MTOTO must go into the record books as an unlucky loser.

MTOTO retired to the Aston Upthorpe Stud in Oxfordshire where he is certain to attract more than his share of blue-blooded mares. Hopefully he will prove to be as successful as his sire Busted, who unfortunately died of a heart attack in March 1988.

# 1988

## KING GEORGE VI AND QUEEN ELIZABETH DIAMOND STAKES (GROUP ONE)

£218,808     1m 4f

July 23, 1988

| 1 | MTOTO | 5 9–7 | M. Roberts. b.h. by Busted–Amazer |
|---|---|---|---|
| 2 | UNFUWAIN (USA) | 3 8–8 | W. Carson. b.c. by Northern Dancer–Height of Fashion |
| 3 | TONY BIN | 5 9–7 | P. Eddery. b.h. by Kampala–Severn Bridge |
| 4 | ALMAARAD | 5 9–7 | S. Cauthen. ch.h. by Ela-Mana-Mou–Silk Blend |
| 5 | PERCY'S LASS | 4 9–4 | Paul Eddery. b.f. by Blakeney–Laughing Girl |
| 6 | DOYOUN | 3 8–8 | W. Swinburn. b.c. by Mill Reef–Dumka |
| 7 | SOFT MACHINE (USA) | 3 8–8 | D. Boeuf. b.c. by Foolish Pleasure–Soft Stepper |
| 8 | GLACIAL STORM (USA) | 3 8–8 | M. Hills. b.c. by Arctic Tern–Hortensia |
| 9 | SILVER LANE (USA) | 3 8–5 | A. Cruz. b.f. by Silver Hawk–Strait Lane |
| 10 | MOON MADNESS | 5 9–7 | T. Ives. b.h. by Vitiges–Castle Moon |

10 Ran

Going – Good to Soft

Distances: 2,1½,1½,3,1½,2½,5

Time: 2:37.33

S.P. 2–1 UNFUWAIN, 4–1 MTOTO, 9–2 TONY BIN, 6–1 GLACIAL STORM, 7–1 DOYOUN, 10–1 ALMAARAD, 33–1 SILVER LANE, 50–1 MOON MADNESS, 66–1 PERCY'S LASS, 200–1 SOFT MACHINE

Winner trained by Alec Stewart at Newmarket: owned by Sheikh Ahmed Al Maktoum: bred by Mr J. L. Moore

Timeform rating of winner 134

# 1989

A feeling of euphoria pervades the winner's enclosure at Newmarket minutes after NASHWAN has made an astonishing seasonal debut by running away with the Two Thousand Guineas. Before a heaving pack of journalists, Major Dick Hern, relishing the sweetness of victory, is holding court. One well-known scribe opens the interrogation.

"How will the colt handle the twists and turns of Epsom?" he asks.

The reply flashes back at him without an instant's hesitation. "He could gallop down the side of a house!" retorts the Major.

At his side, the normally talkative Willie Carson can hardly get a word in edgeways as the Master of West Ilsley entertains the assembled hacks. For the wheelchair-bound Major, NASHWAN's victory is more than a Classic success. It is a superbly timed demonstration of his ability to practise his craft to the highest standards in the face of mounting pressure to retire.

Storm clouds had been fast gathering over West Ilsley in the recent past. The Major had first of all suffered a crippling injury in a hunting accident and then he had developed a debilitating heart condition. Finally, he had been given notice to quit from the stables he had commanded with such success for nearly thirty years. Yet from the midst of this gathering gloom, there had emerged a shining beacon of hope, carrying the blue and white silks of Sheikh Hamdan Al Maktoum.

The long hot summer of 1989 brought conclusive evidence of the maturity of the Maktoum family's breeding empire. NASHWAN, the record-breaking winner of the Two Thousand Guineas, the Derby, the Eclipse and the King George was out of Sheikh Hamdan's celebrated mare Height of Fashion. Already the dam of the useful Alwasmi and the more than useful Unfuwain, Height of Fashion must now be acclaimed as one of the most remarkable brood mares of the past century.

In appearance NASHWAN, a most imposing chestnut with a tremendous stride, was not unlike his sire Blushing Groom. He made his racecourse debut in the Yattendon Stakes over seven furlongs at Newbury. Despite running green, he won as he liked, striding home three parts of a length clear of his closest pursuer.

After Newbury, NASHWAN developed a slight foot injury which prevented his participation in the Royal Lodge Stakes. Having made a full recovery, Major Hern's colt contested the Red Oaks Autumn Stakes over the Ascot mile. Sent off the 4–6 favourite, he retained his unbeaten record with a smooth four-length victory over Optimist. In third place that day, five and a half lengths off the winner, came a colt making his racecourse debut. His name was Cacoethes.

NASHWAN was obviously a horse with vast potential, and so the ever-patient Hern decided to put him away for the winter after his Ascot victory. His two wins had earned him a rating of eight stone, three pounds in the European Free Handicap, eighteen pounds below Henry Cecil's High Estate.

In the week leading up to the Two Thousand Guineas, the world and his wife seemed to have heard about a remarkable piece of work which had taken place on Newbury racecourse. Apparently NASHWAN had not only outstripped the local pigeon population, he had left them for dead in his slipstream. The bookmakers were bombarded with enquiries about just one Guineas contender – NASHWAN. Three weeks prior to the race he had been a 33–1 chance; on the day he started favourite at 3–1.

In the event, NASHWAN proved to be the most eloquent "talking horse" for many a year. Under an inspired ride from Willie Carson, the chestnut flashed like a streak of lightning inside the final furlong to win the fastest ever electronically recorded Two Thousand Guineas in history. The feat was all the more meritorious as NASHWAN, in common with Hern's 1971 Two Thousand Guineas winner Brigadier Gerard, did not have the benefit of a prep-race.

NASHWAN looked a champion in the making at Newmarket, yet even his most vociferous supporters were left gasping for breath after the colt had slaughtered the opposition in the Epsom Derby, to give Sheikh Hamdan his first Blue Riband. Treating the tricky Epsom bends with the utmost ease, NASHWAN cruised into the lead below the distance and soon had his opponents toiling in his wake. Cacoethes, considered by his connections to be the equal of Dancing Brave at home, had no answer to NASHWAN's blinding acceleration up the straight and was beaten fully two furlongs out. Although the 500–1 outsider Terimon ran on well in the closing stages, at the post it was a case of NASHWAN first, the rest nowhere.

With Sheikh Mohammed's Old Vic adding the Irish Derby to his earlier success in the French equivalent, the Maktoum star was very much in the ascendant during the summer months. A match between the two Derby winners would have been a prospect to savour, but unfortunately it was destined never to be. After his Curragh victory, Old Vic was forced to the sidelines by illness.

Despite persistent worries about a poisoned foot, NASHWAN was able to meet his next engagement in the Coral Eclipse Stakes at Sandown. Taking on his elders for the first time, he became the first horse since Blue Peter in 1939 to win the Two Thousand Guineas, the Derby, and the Eclipse in the same season. Three furlongs out, however, those who had laid the odds on NASHWAN must have been having severe palpitations as the dual Classic winner was fully eight lengths behind the pacemaker Opening Verse. In a matter of strides, however, Carson had turned the deficit into a five-length advantage over the Cecil-trained colt. With older horses of the calibre of Indian Skimmer and Warning in rear, this was a performance of the highest class.

The racing public love an unbeaten champion, and in NASHWAN they had a colt who appeared to have the potential to fight off all challengers. The King George was next on the agenda and the Diamonds looked destined for Dubai.

Guy Harwood, still smarting from Cacoethes's Epsom defeat, was determined to prove that his colt was better than his Derby form. The son of Alydar, formerly lumbered with the horrendous name, My Friend Elvis, had returned to winning ways after Epsom with a workmanlike success in the King Edward VII Stakes at Royal Ascot. Hopes were high at Pulborough that the American-bred bay would prove a worthy opponent for NASHWAN in the King George.

Of the remaining five challengers, Coronation Cup and Grand Prix de Paris winner Sheriff's Star appeared the most likely to cause an upset, although Michael Jarvis's Carroll House was quietly fancied in Newmarket.

Diamond Day 1989 was one of the hottest on record and afternoon temperatures hovered around the nineties. The glorious weather and the presence of NASHWAN combined to attract a mammoth attendance of over thirty thousand spectators to the Berkshire track.

Not surprisingly, all seven King George contestants became extremely warm during the preliminaries, each arriving down at the start lathered in sweat. After being loaded into the stalls with the minimum of fuss, the field were despatched by starter Captain Brown.

NASHWAN's connections had taken the precaution of running a pacemaker, Polemos, in order to ensure a true gallop. Richard Hills duly sent his mount into the lead from the break, but to the amazement of most observers, he then proceeded to set only a moderate pace which in effect turned the race into a tactical battle of wits over the first mile and a sprint for glory over the final four furlongs.

Behind the leader, the two principals, NASHWAN and Cacoethes, were playing a game of cat and mouse, while Carson and Starkey watched each other like hawks. As Polemos dropped away four furlongs out, Michael Roberts sent his mount Top Class scuttling into the lead in an effort to catch the two market leaders flat-footed. Turning into the straight, Top Class was being vigorously ridden to maintain his advantage, but unfortunately for Roberts, inescapable Fate was pounding ever closer.

One and a half out NASHWAN loomed up alongside the leader, who, under severe pressure from his pilot, veered sharply left, bumping his challenger in the process. For a few heart-stopping seconds NASHWAN lost his momentum and Carson was forced to utilise all his considerable experience in an effort to revive his hampered mount. Proving that he had the courage to match his brilliance, NASHWAN rallied magnificently in the manner of a true champion. In a matter of strides the giant chestnut forged past his wayward rival, soon leaving him for dead.

While this drama had been unfolding, Cacoethes had been making relentless progress from the rear of the field. As he cruised up alongside NASHWAN inside the final furlong, thirty thousand spectators rose as one to cheer home the two warriors.

A battle of epic proportions began to develop as the two principals pulled away from the rest of the field. With a hundred yards to run it was neck and neck, no quarter given, no quarter asked. Both jockeys rode to the wire as if the devil were on their heels, their whips rising and falling almost in unison. Only in the very last strides did NASHWAN's chestnut head inch its way in front of his gallant rival, the pair flashing past the post locked together in blood-stirring combat. The Derby winner had maintained his unbeaten record, but only by the length of his blue-blooded neck.

The 1989 King George will be remembered by all those fortunate enough to have witnessed it as the greatest flat race to have taken place on British soil since Grundy's record-breaking run for the Diamonds in 1975. NASHWAN's thrilling victory earned him a place in racing's Hall of Fame as the only horse ever to win the Two Thousand Guineas, Derby, Eclipse and King George in the same season.

Hamdan Al Maktoum's champion was now syndicated at a value of £18 million, with his owner retaining a majority holding.

Two possible targets lay open to NASHWAN after Ascot – a tilt at the Prix de l'Arc de Triomphe or an attempt at the elusive Triple Crown, by way of victory in the St Leger. His trainer favoured the latter plan, but was overruled by Sheikh Hamdan who preferred the trip to Longchamp.

The Prix Niel was chosen as NASHWAN's preparation for the Arc. The Group Two race over the Arc course and distance was expected to be little more than an exercise canter for the King George hero. In the event the race produced possibly the greatest upset of the decade when NASHWAN lost his unbeaten record in sensational fashion, beaten not just by one horse, but by two. On ground much softer than he liked, NASHWAN ran a lifeless race to be beaten by one and a half lengths and half a length by the French-trained pair, Golden Pheasant and French Glory.

A lengthy series of tests failed to solve the mystery of NASHWAN's sensational defeat and after much deliberation it was decided to bypass the Arc. Carroll House, beaten over eleven lengths at Ascot, scored a remarkable victory at Longchamp, giving Newmarket trainer Michael Jarvis the most prestigious success of his career.

NASHWAN's farewell appearance was rescheduled and the eyes of the expectant racing world turned to Newmarket and the Dubai Champion Stakes. But once again, the gods intervened. On the Tuesday prior to the race, Major Hern issued a statement which reported that NASHWAN was found to have a temperature of 102 and as a result he would be unable to fulfil his intended engagement. So Sheikh Hamdan's magnificent chestnut, his reputation tarnished by that single defeat, was retired without a chance to vindicate himself before the increasing number of his critics.

The bitter pill of NASHWAN's retirement was considerably sweetened by the news that he was to stand on this side of the Atlantic at his owner's Shadwell Stud complex. On pedigree, race-course performance and looks, NASHWAN has all the credentials necessary to be a runaway success as a stallion. His first progeny are awaited with excitement and keen anticipation.

NASHWAN was unarguably a true champion. It takes a horse of outstanding quality to rewrite the record books as NASHWAN did in 1989. Although he failed to maintain his unbeaten record, prior to his defeat in Paris the colt had produced a series of outstanding performances at eight, ten and twelve furlongs, culminating in his sparkling King George victory on that unforgettable Saturday in July.

## 1989

### KING GEORGE VI AND QUEEN ELIZABETH DIAMOND STAKES (GROUP ONE)

£218,088    1m 4f

July 22, 1989

| | | | |
|---|---|---|---|
| 1 NASHWAN (USA) | 3 8–8 | W. Carson. ch.c. by Blushing Groom–Height of Fashion |
| 2 CACOETHES (USA) | 3 8–8 | G. Starkey. b.c. by Alydar–Careless Notion |
| 3 TOP CLASS | 4 9–7 | M. Roberts. b.c. by High Top–Cassina |
| 4 SHERIFF'S STAR | 4 9–7 | T. Ives. gr.c. by Posse–Castle Moon |
| 5 CARROLL HOUSE | 4 9–7 | W. Swinburn. ch.c. by Lord Gayle–Tuna |
| 6 POLEMOS | 5 9–7 | R. Hills. ch.h. by Formidable–Polemia |
| 7 TISSERAND (ITY) | 4 9–7 | L. Sorrentino. gr.c. by Nadjar–Tandina |

7 Ran

Going – Good to Firm

Distances: nk,7,1,3,1½,¾

Time: 2:32.27

S.P. 2–9 NASHWAN, 6–I CACOETHES, IO–I SHERIFF'S STAR, 33–I CARROLL HOUSE, 50–I TOP CLASS, TISSERAND, 500–I POLEMOS

Winner trained by Major Hern at West Ilsley: owned by Sheikh Hamdan Al Maktoum: bred by owner

Timeform rating of winner 135

# BIBLIOGRAPHY

Baerlein, Richard: *Nijinski, Triple Crown Winner*; Pelham, London, 1971.
—— *Joe Mercer*; Macdonald, London, 1987.
Biographical Encyclopedia of British Flat Racing (Mortimer, Onslow, Willett); Macdonald & James, London, 1978.
Breasley, Scobie & Poole, Christopher: *Scobie*; Macdonald, London, 1984.
Carr, Harry: *Queen's Jockey*; Stanley Paul, London, 1966.
Curling, Bill: *The Captain*; Barrie & Jenkins, London, 1970.
David, Roy: *The Shergar Mystery*; Trainer's Record, Dorset, 1986.
Devonshire, 11th Duke of, Andrew. *Park Top*; London Magazine Editions, London 1976.
Fitzgeorge-Parker, Tim: *Grundy*; W. H. Allen, London, 1976.
—— *The Guvnor*; Collins, London, 1980.
Fitzgerald, Arthur: *Prix de l'Arc de Triomphe 1965–82*; Sidgewick & Jackson, London, 1983.
Francis, Dick: *Lester*; Michael Joseph, 1986.
Hawkins, Christopher: *The Race of the Century*; Allen & Unwin, London, 1976.
Marsh, Marcus: *Racing with the Gods*; Pelham, London, 1968.
Oaksey, John: *The Story of Mill Reef*; Michael Joseph, London, 1974.
Raceform Annuals
Richards, Sir Gordon: *My Story*; Hodder & Stoughton, London, 1955.
Seth-Smith, Michael: *Bred for The Purple*; Leslie Frewin, London, 1969.
—— *Knight of the Turf*; Hodder & Stoughton, London, 1980.
Smirke, Charlie: *Finishing Post*; Oldbourne Book Co., London, 1960.
Timeform's *Racehorses* Annuals.